PROPHECY'S LIGHT ON TODAY

Rev H. H. Vine.

Read and Return

PROPHECY'S LIGHT ON TODAY

By

CHARLES G. TRUMBULL, Litt.D.

44218

INTRODUCTION BY

HOWARD A. KELLY, M.D., LL.D.

W. W. Vine
516 - 6 St S.W. Rochester,
Minn.

NEW YORK

Fleming H. Revell Company

LONDON AND EDINBURGH

Pearlman Memorial Library
Central Bible College
Springfield, Missouri

New York: 158 Fifth Avenue
London: 21 Paternoster Square

FOREWORD

MOST of the chapters of this volume appeared as a series of articles in *The Sunday School Times* during 1937, and are brought together here by permission of The Sunday School Times Company, Philadelphia. Much additional material, however, has now been included which has not been published before in connection with Bible prophecy. The closing section of the book, "Criticisms, Questions, and Testimonies," contains letters from readers of *The Sunday School Times,* with editorial answers, appearing originally in "Notes on Open Letters" in that periodical. A small part of the material in the book appeared in a chapter by the author in a volume entitled *Unveiling the Future,* published by Fundamental Truth Publishers, Findlay, Ohio, and is used by their permission.

The author has had opportunities of speaking on these subjects at conferences in Washington, D. C., on the Pacific Coast at Los Angeles, Pasadena, Glendale, and Mount Hermon, and at the annual Prophetical Conference in Knox Church, Toronto; and he has noted a deepening interest in Bible prophecy, in view of world-shaking current events, among Christian people and others who, until recent years, have had little interest in the subject.

C. G. T.

INTRODUCTION

I WAS brought up on the Second Coming, in the Epiphany Episcopal Church under Dr. Richard Newton, of Philadelphia, who yearly had his pulpit filled by a converted Jew named Newman who discoursed on the return of the Jews to their own land in fulfillment of prophecy. This was in the seventies of the last century. Somehow neither Mr. Newman nor his subject appealed to us. We saw no evidence of any movements of the Jews about us going away, and from what we heard of the land it was a dry, barren place, and the Dead Sea was about the deadest spot in the world, well meriting its name.

And now what? Presto, all is changed! The Jews are flocking or rather being driven back in unbelief in their prophetic Scriptures, and the land is being miraculously transformed: business is flourishing; the Jordan River is harnessed to supply power and electric light; the great port Haifa is established in the old Asher territory with oil flowing in through pipes crossing the desert; Tel Aviv has appeared as a beautiful Jewish city; the soil is productive and quantities of oranges are exported to distant parts; and as for the worthless Dead Sea, its stored up values of bromine and potash are being recovered by plants already erected, with new ones going up, the recoverable potash being sufficient to supply all the world needs for two hundred years in the absence of any other source!

So I have believed in our Lord's Second Coming practically all of my life, but, alas, it was only a documentary belief like the things we sometimes recite in a creed in church on Sunday mornings. And yet the belief did gain a hold upon me, for I held it for some years as a shibboleth dividing the growing and informed from the uninformed and drifting Christians—really a wrong spiritual attitude, to be confessed and overcome. I thought enough of it also to mark every reference to the Second Coming in my Bible

7

with a blue penciled capital A in the margin to facilitate its study.

In the fall of 1936 Mr. Trumbull asked me to write for *The Sunday School Times* on the subject, so I went to work, and listed all the significant passages; but when the outline was finished I laid it aside, as it appeared to me that it had all been said so often in the same way that it was too trite.

And now there arrives this splendid, fresh, informative study, so happily illustrated: full of precious teachings so admirably presented, making one eager to send the work to one's friends. Such a prayerful study does this call for, fixing one's thoughts on the great, legitimate hope of our age—our Lord's Return to reign in righteousness. It becomes a happy sort of pessimistic-optimism; for if the last dreadful evil days are now running their course, destined to end in the speedy return of our Lord, surely that is the highest sort of optimism. While, if men by the socialization of the Church and Society are to transform the world (the so-called optimistic view), what ages of waiting will this call for in view of our present status after these nineteen hundred years!

One's interest in the narrative is further greatly enhanced by a warm sense of a personal companionship with one who so freely and frankly confesses his original difficulties in accepting the truth of a Second Coming as an antecedent to Christ's millennial reign.

What a lesson, too, the writer has taught me in recording that remark of my old friend Dr. Gray, to the effect that, "When a Christian discovers the indwelling Christ, he soon begins to discover the returning Christ." Is it not a great, obvious, important truth that we cannot grow into a living apprehension of more advanced truths until we have fully apprehended the antecedent underlying basic truths?

First, the Virgin Birth of the Son of God—Son of Man; then His sacrificial life and crucifixion; then His resurrection and ascension; to be followed by His glorious return, to reign with His saints, to the world where He was so dishonored. Who will worry, or who will not rather give thanks, that our Father is clearly guiding all things to a determined end such as we anticipate in Ephesians, Colos-

sians, and Revelation? Without this doctrine the faith of
many must collapse; with it, faith becomes invigorated and
the vision infinitely enlarged.

The whole world of nature appears in our day to be in
revolt, with all her unprecedented disturbances. And how
clearly are the nations preparing by granting unrestrained
powers to individual men, such as we note in Russia,
Germany, Italy, and in our own country,—all preparing for
the one man prophesied by our Lord in John 5:43:
"I am come in my Father's name, and ye receive Me
not: if another shall come in his own name, him ye will
receive." We are surely in the world-age of the feet of
iron mixed with miry clay of Daniel's image.

Let me repeat that this book, so full of spiritual meat
and helpful, illustrative anecdotes, so interesting while so
splendidly setting forth these vital, scattered Bible teachings, is destined to reach many hearts and to build up many
Christians in a more vital, Spirit-filled faith.

HOWARD A. KELLY

Baltimore, Md.

CONTENTS

CRITICISMS, QUESTIONS, AND TESTIMONIES

I

THE SHARP SWORD OF PROPHECY

DIVINE prophecy has cut deep into men's lives from the days before the Flood, even in the garden of Eden, until today—and it is still doing so. Prophecy was the keen-cutting test of men at the time of Christ's first advent: it is the same inescapable test today as his Second Coming draws nigh. It tested and sifted and blessed and condemned men during the thousands of years before Christ's first coming; it will continue to test and sift men after His Second Coming, during and at the end of the Millennium of His reign on earth (Rev. 13; 20:7-9).

Prophecy is the sharpest of all swords, because it is "the sword of the Spirit, which is the word of God" (Eph. 6:17), and "the word of God is living, and powerful, and sharper than any twoedged sword, piercing even to the dividing asunder of soul and spirit, and of the joints and marrow, and is a discerner [critic, or judge] of the thoughts and intents of the heart" (Heb. 4:12). Scriptural prophecy is infallible, "for the prophecy came not in old time by the will of man: but holy men of God spake as they were moved by the Holy Ghost" (2 Pet. 1:21).

Prophecy is not only contained in the Word of God, but it seems safe to say that the Bible is chiefly a Book of Prophecy. Prophecy is its diapason, its great, dominant note from Genesis to Revelation. Let us not forget that all the precious promises of God which shine through the Scriptures are prophecies, as well as all the other predictive Scriptures. God's promises and prophecies include solemn warnings and inescapable judgments, as well as gracious assurances of His infinite love and mercy. It is plain, therefore, that the sharp sword of divine prophecy is the perpetual test of men during this present life. It tests the unsaved; it tests the saved. God's own people have missed many blessings, which He has longed to give them, because they would not believe certain of His prophecies.

Divine prophecy began in the second chapter of Genesis. The prophecy test began then, and in the next chapter man failed to meet the test. In his perfect environment of Eden, in his sinlessness and fellowship with God, being made in the image of God, Adam was given every blessing and liberty to enjoy all this to the uttermost, but with the divine prophecy, given in loving warning not to eat of a certain tree: *"for in the day that thou eatest thereof thou shalt surely die."*

The federal head of the human race failed to meet the prophecy test, and he brought ruin and death to all mankind by this failure.

But God's prophecies had only begun. In the third chapter of Genesis came the precious prophecy of redemption through the seed of the woman (Gen. 3:15). The first prophecy was a warning of death. The second prophecy, a promise of life.

And so started the gulf stream of Bible prophecy, continuing ever wider, fuller, and deeper throughout the sacred writings, until the last and sixty-sixth book, Revelation, the greatest of all the prophetic Scriptures, closes with the blessed prophecy from the lips of the Son of God, "Surely I come quickly."

Adam was the first man, but not the last, who failed to meet the prophecy test. All through Old Testament times there were those who refused to believe God's prophecies, and who suffered unspeakably because of this. But the inspired history shines out with the record of many others who took God at His word, believed His prophecies, and enjoyed unspeakable blessing.

The prophecy of the Flood was such a test. The unsaved world refused to believe the prophecy and went down in destruction. In contrast, "By faith Noah, being warned of God of things not seen as yet, moved with fear, prepared an ark to the saving of his house; by the which he condemned the world, and became heir of the righteousness which is by faith" (Heb. 11:7).

Some sixteen centuries later a prophet of God named

Jonah went to one of the great cities of ancient civilization, Nineveh, godless, pagan, and wicked, and proclaimed God's prophecy: "Yet forty days, and Nineveh shall be overthrown" (Jonah 3:4). All the people of Nineveh, from the king on his throne to his lowliest subject, believed God, and met the prophecy test by repenting in sackcloth and ashes. They cried "mightily unto God," and God heard them, rejoiced in their repentance, and delivered that great city from His destroying judgment.

History repeated itself in New Testament times, and is repeating itself today; some believe God's prophecies, some —even among God's own people—fail before the prophecy test and miss the blessing that might be theirs.

A dozen years ago a well known Presbyterian minister and editor, not now living, made a visit to one of the summer conferences at Stony Brook, Long Island, and wrote for his own paper an account of his impressions. He congratulated Dr. Carson, then at the head of Stony Brook Assembly, "on the great work he is doing," but went on to speak sharply of what he considered the great blemish in Stony Brook's ministry: its interest in the return of the Lord. Said he:

> As to the Second Coming of Christ nobody knows anything about it; it is impossible to tell just what the writers of the New Testament themselves believed; it looks as if Paul himself changed his mind about it; equally good men hold utterly varying views about it; it does not seem to have any effect upon character one way or another, as half the saints believe in it and half do not; and *what difference does it make, anyhow?*

It is difficult to believe that this could come from the heart and mind of a professing minister of the Gospel; yet there are many others, in the ministry and in our theological seminaries as well as in the rank and file of our churches, who would say that this view is their ov n.

God forbid that we should fail to meet the prophecy test in that way! Have we realized that the Holy Spirit has given "that blessed hope" of the Second Coming of Christ far more prominence and more frequent mention than any other doctrine in the entire Bible, from Genesis to Revelation? It is referred to more than three hundred times in the New Testament, and Paul in his inspired (God-breathed) writings could no more have "changed his mind about it" than could the Holy Spirit. In four of the last Epistles he wrote, in his old age, Paul said, for example:

For our conversation [citizenship] is in heaven; *from whence also we look for the Saviour,* the Lord Jesus Christ: who shall change our vile body, that it may be fashioned like unto his glorious body (Phil. 3:20, 21).

That thou keep this commandment without spot, unrebukable, *until the appearing* of our Lord Jesus Christ (1 Tim. 6: 14).

Henceforth there is laid up for me a crown of righteousness, . . . and not to me only, but unto all them also *that love his appearing* (2 Tim. 4: 8).

We should live soberly, righteously, and godly, in this present world; *looking for that blessed hope, and the glorious appearing* of the great God and our Saviour Jesus Christ (Titus 2:12, 13).

It is refreshing to turn from that sad testimony of a Presbyterian minister who failed to meet the prophecy test, and read a letter that recently came to *The Sunday School Times* from another minister. He tells of having lived sixty-two years without the Blessed Hope, and what its "discovery" means to him now:

I am an old man who has passed his seventy-sixth birthday last December (1935). I am a retired minister of the Gospel of the grace of God,—have been in the ministry for forty-three years.

I never knew what the premillenarian doctrine was until twelve years ago this winter, and I accepted it at once. It has been such an uplift for me spiritually that my joy in the Blessed Hope has wonderfully influenced my life. And now I thank the Lord that my eyes have been opened, and that I see the truth as I never did before.

And now, as the sunset of my life is near, and I look to the hills toward the western horizon, the future looks as bright as the promises of God, and they are surely wonderful

Yes, the promises and prophecies of God are indeed "surely wonderful." Why are they not believed? Why do so many fail to meet the prophecy test?

Perhaps men may be divided into two general classes in thinking of this question.

There are those who reject the Bible as God's inspired and infallible Word, and therefore who have no difficulty in throwing out, as unreliable and not to be given serious attention, any part of it that does not accord with their own "better judgment," and especially the prophecies.

The other class is more difficult to understand: it includes God's own people, true believers and children of God, who nevertheless for one reason or another, like the disciples themselves and this minister who, in spite of his true Christian belief and Bible study, failed to see the truth of certain prophecies until late in life, have heard and read and studied certain plain prophecies but have not taken in their real meaning.

The eleven true and believing apostles of our Lord were in this class; and many of us know only too well, out of our own experience, what an "apostolic succession" there has been within the true Church of Christ from their day until now.

The apostles suffered needless discouragement, heartbreak, agony of spirit because they failed to meet the prophecy test at the time of Christ's crucifixion. Had they intelligently taken in, and really believed, the prophecies that Christ had given them plainly and repeatedly about His coming death and resurrection, there would have been no such breakdown of their faith as the Gospels record when prophecy was fulfilled, and their Lord's Messiahship was confirmed and credentialed, by His crucifixion and resurrection.

Failing to meet the prophecy test, the disciples lost all hope when He was crucified; and they would not believe that He had risen from the dead.

But *could* they have understood the Old Testament prophecies of these inescapable and assured events had they been more faithful and devoted in listening to the Word of God? Or was it impossible for them to understand until after the events had taken place?

We need be in no doubt as to the answer, for it comes from the Lord Himself. He never would have rebuked the disciples whom He joined on the way to Emmaus if they had been blameless. After listening patiently to their narrative of the crucifixion, and of the collapse of their hopes:

Then he said unto them, O fools [foolish ones], and slow of heart to believe all that the prophets have spoken: ought not Christ to have suffered these things, and to enter into his glory? And beginning at Moses and all the prophets, he expounded unto them in all the scriptures the things concerning himself (Luke 24:25-27).

Later that night, when these two had returned to Jerusalem and joined the eleven, and when the risen Lord had appeared to them all, and they, still failing to meet the prophecy test, were first terrified and then "believed not for joy," the Lord had more to say to them about prophecy. First He patiently proved to them that He was not a spirit, a ghost, but their own Messiah and Lord, risen in His own body. Then He said:

These are the words which I spake unto you, while I was yet with you, that all things must be fulfilled, which were written in the law of Moses, and in the prophets, and in the psalms, concerning me. Then opened he their understanding, that they might understand the scriptures (Luke 24:44, 45).

All that was needed to enable God's people to recognize their Messiah when He came was plainly given in Old Testament prophecies. Outstanding among the facts and events thus predicted of His first advent are the following:

The Place of His Birth.

His Virgin Birth.

His Deity.

His Sacrificial Death and Blood Atonement.

His Bodily Resurrection.

These prophecies, and the New Testament Scriptures recording their fulfillment, are worth noting carefully, as follows:

The Bethlehem Birth:
  Prophecy: Micah 5:2.
  Fulfillment: Matthew 2:1-6.

The Virgin Birth:
  Prophecy: Isaiah 7:14.
  Fulfillment: Matthew 1:18-23.

The Deity of the Messiah:
  Prophecy: Isaiah 9:6, 7.
  Fulfillment: John 20:28, 29.

The Substitutionary Death:
  Prophecy: Isaiah 53—which has been called "the blue-
  print of the New Testament."
  Fulfillment: John 1:29 with 1 Peter 2:24.
  There are, of course, many other Old and New
  Testament Scriptures giving this prophecy and this
  fulfillment; such as Psalm 22 with 2 Corinthians 5:21.

The Bodily Resurrection:
  Prophecy: Psalm 16:10.
  Fulfillment: Acts 2:25-31.

It has been noted that there are no less than twenty-five
Old Testament prophecies bearing on the betrayal, trial,
death, and burial of the Lord Jesus Christ, uttered by many
different voices during the five centuries from 1000 to
500 B.C., which were all literally fulfilled within twenty-four
hours at the time of His crucifixion. Truly, God did not
leave either His own people or the unsaved world without
abundant witness to all that they needed to know, both for
salvation and for peace of mind and joy of heart.

God's own people were tested by prophecy at the time
of the first advent of Christ, even as they are being similarly
tested today when His Second Coming is so near at hand.
Some failed to meet the test; some met it gloriously.

Paul told of the failure to meet the test when he declared
to the Jews in the synagogue at Antioch in Pisidia: "For
they that dwell at Jerusalem, and their rulers, because they
knew him [Jesus Christ] not, nor yet the voices of the
prophets which are read every sabbath day, they have fulfilled them in condemning him" (Acts 13:27).

The aged priest Zacharias, although he had his moment
of wavering in faith, nevertheless rejoiced in his knowledge
of, and belief in, Old Testament prophecy and so met the

test triumphantly as he was given the great privilege of becoming the father of John the Baptist. See Luke 1:5, 6, 17, 67-75; with Malachi 3:1; 4:2, 5, 6.

The aged Simeon met the test, with great thanksgiving and joy. See Luke 2:25-32; with Isaiah 42:6, 7.

The aged Anna, herself a prophetess, had studied Old Testament prophecy and thus met the test when the babe Messiah came (Luke 2:36-38).

We do not always remember that Joseph of Arimathea, who "had not consented" to the Sanhedrin's verdict against Christ, and who fulfilled prophecy by his loving and reverent burial of the body of our Lord, had been enlightened by his study of prophecy, for he "also himself waited for the kingdom of God" (Luke 23:51).

The tragedy of failing to meet the prophecy test is that those who thus fail are themselves unconsciously fulfilling prophecy. In an article published in the *Atlantic Monthly* in 1923, the late Dr. George A. Gordon, pastor of the Old South Church of Boston, wrote these strange words:

> In these days, among ourselves, certain writers and speakers hotly affirm as fundamentals what no reasonable man can believe—the absence of error from the books of the Old and New Testaments, the necessity of expiation in order to be forgiven, the dependence of the future life for man upon reunion with the body vacated at death, and the return of Jesus of Nazareth in the flesh, no longer as Saviour but as Judge. One may sympathize deeply with the zeal of these persons, even praise their passionate desire to vindicate what they believe to be true, and yet hold that the ideas cited are not only wanting in the character of fundamentals but that *they are simple foolishness* (italics ours).

Here is fulfilled prophecy. For nineteen centuries before this "exposure" of "simple foolishness" appeared in a magazine of the intelligentsia, God declared that "after that in the wisdom of God the world by wisdom knew not God, it pleased God by the foolishness of preaching [the thing preached] to save them that believe." "Christ crucified" is "unto the Greeks foolishness. . . . Because the foolishness of God is wiser than men" (1 Cor. 1:21-25).

And another prophecy that many are unconsciously fulfilling today in their rejection of prophecy is that of Peter's inspired writing:

Knowing this first, that there shall come in the last days scoffers, walking after their own lusts, and saying, Where is the promise of his coming? for since the fathers fell asleep, all things continue as they were from the beginning of the creation (2 Pet. 3:3, 4).

May God grant that we shall not fail before the test of prophecy.

II

THE BIBLE'S VERDICT

WHILE in the Far East some years ago, I asked a missionary in Seoul whether the Korean Christians believed in the Second Coming of Christ. "Oh, yes," he answered; "they believe the Bible. It is only when some missionaries come and tell them something different that they begin to have any doubts."

This missionary felt—as do many others—that to open the Bible and read it with an open mind and heart can have only one result; unquestioning acceptance of God's plain declaration that His Son, the Lord Jesus Christ, is coming again to this earth to establish His Kingdom here.

At a missionary conference in America, a few years earlier, I had met a missionary from India. We fell into conversation about the Second Coming of Christ, and he told me his experience.

He had gone to India fresh from a conservative theological seminary, convinced that the Lord would not return until after the Church had Christianized the world. In his mission station in India were some English women missionaries who were ardent premillenarians. When they found what his views were, they started in with zeal to show him his mistake. There were lengthy and rather heated arguments, back and forth. The women missionaries plied him with Scripture passages to prove that the Kingdom could not come on earth until the King had returned. The American missionary was quite unconvinced, but he could not prove his position to their satisfaction. And he was bothered by the fact that he could not quote Scripture on his side as readily and freely as they were doing on theirs.

So he determined to close their mouths and put an end to the argument by using their own weapon, the Bible. But he realized that he must do this thoroughly and convincingly, if he was to do it at all. He was unwilling to do it superficially, so he started in in dead earnest.

He took his Bible, and he took notebooks, and he read the Scriptures thoroughly and carefully, in order to set down in one grouping all the Scriptures he could find that proved his position—that Christ would not come again until after the world was converted. With equal honesty he determined to set down any passages he might find that seemed to show that the other view, held by the English missionaries, was the correct one.

After some months of close study he told his missionary friends that he was now ready to talk the matter over with them again, and do so on their own ground—that of the Bible. "But," said the American missionary, "having finished my study of the Bible on this subject, I find I am entirely in agreement with you!" He had discovered that there is only one answer in the Scriptures.

The American missionary was now a convinced pre-millenarian. He had done what few who do not look for the Lord's return before the millennium ever do: he had really studied the whole Bible to see what it has to say on the subject. Like the Korean Christians, he really believed the Bible, and he found that the Second Coming of Christ to end the age in which we are now living, and in which both the world and the professing Christian Church will have gone down in failure and defeat, is unmistakably declared and is our sure and blessed hope.

We may safely say, therefore, that the *first reason why we should believe in the Second Coming of Christ is because the Bible says He is coming again.* The Second Coming is the most prominent theme, next to Christ Himself, in the entire Bible. Throughout the Old Testament and the New it is presented far oftener than any other doctrine.

Among the more than three hundred New Testament passages on the Lord's return, the seven following are typical:

For the Son of man is as a man taking a far journey, who left his house, and gave authority to his servants, and to every man his work, and commanded the porter to watch. Watch ye therefore: for ye know not when the master of the house cometh, at even, or at midnight, or at the cockcrowing, or in the morning: lest coming suddenly he find you sleeping. ' And what I say unto you I say unto all, Watch (Mark 13:34-37).

I go to prepare a place for you. And if I go and prepare a place for you, I will come again, and receive you unto myself (John 14:2, 3).

For as the lightning cometh out of the east, and shineth even unto the west; so shall also the coming of the Son of man be (Matt. 24:27).

This same Jesus, which is taken up from you into heaven, shall so come in like manner as ye have seen him go into heaven (Acts 1:11).

So Christ was once offered to bear the sins of many; and unto them that look for him shall he appear the second time without sin unto salvation (Heb. 9:28).

For as often as ye eat this bread, and drink this cup, ye do shew the Lord's death till he come (1 Cor. 11:26).

For the grace of God that bringeth salvation hath appeared to all men, teaching us that, denying ungodliness and worldly lusts, we should live soberly, righteously, and godly, in this present world; looking for that blessed hope, and the glorious appearing of the great God and our Saviour Jesus Christ (Titus 2:11-13).

It is true that there are devout Christian people, born-again children of God, who believe the Scriptures unquestioningly and yet who do not accept the premillennial return of the Lord as a Scriptural doctrine. But usually, when such a believer is asked what his view of Christ's return is, he will answer, "I really have not studied that subject closely." If all those who question or deny the Lord's return as the only way by which the millennium, or His Kingdom, is to be established on earth, would do as the honest missionary in India did, there would surely be a great increase in the number of those who are "looking for that blessed hope, and the glorious appearing of the great God and our Saviour Jesus Christ" (Titus 2:13).

The Bible tells us that we ought to be looking for the Lord's return. Dr. A. J. Gordon, of blessed ministry and beloved memory, made an illuminating comment on the word of the two angels to the disciples who "looked stedfastly toward heaven as he [Christ] went up" from them in His ascension. We are told that "two men stood by them in white apparel," and that these men asked a question of the disciples: "Ye men of Galilee, why stand ye gazing up into heaven?"

We mistakenly think, said Dr. Gordon, that the angels were rebuking the disciples by their question. The question was not a rebuke, but was asked in order to introduce the divine explanation of what the disciples were doing. That is, it was as though the angels said to the disciples something like this: "You are gazing up into heaven, as you ought to do; but you do not know why you are doing so, and we will tell you: 'this same Jesus, which is taken up from you into heaven, shall so come in like manner as ye have seen him go into heaven'" (Acts 1:11).

The angels' question, therefore, was not a rebuke but an explanation. The disciples were right in having the upward heavenly look at that time, and from that time on; and the only true and right attitude of the Church of Christ from that day to this is the attitude of "gazing up into heaven" in eager, assured knowledge that the Lord Who ascended is coming again.

And when He comes again it will be in triumph, not in humiliation. God's eternal purpose includes two notable entries for His Son into Jerusalem, as King of the Jews. One of these occurred nineteen centuries ago, and is commonly called the triumphal entry; Matthew tells us that the Lord fulfilled the prophecy in Zechariah 9:9, which tells Jerusalem to rejoice because "thy King cometh unto thee: he is just, and having salvation; lowly, and riding upon an ass, and upon a colt the foal of an ass." While the multitude did indeed shout, "Hosanna to the son of David," it was far from being a triumphal entry, for the same multitude was soon shouting, "Crucify him." Our Lord's use of the ass, the lowly beast of burden, was undoubtedly symbolic of His coming then, as Zechariah prophesied, to bring salvation rather than judgment; peace for those who would accept their peace with God through Him, rather than war. As Matthew Henry comments: "Horses were kept only by great men, and for war. Christ could have summoned a cherub to carry him (Psa. 18:10); but though by his name Jah, which speaks him God, he rides upon the heavens, yet now by his name Jesus Immanuel, God with us, in his state of humiliation he rides upon an ass." The really triumphal entry is yet to come, and the King then will not ride upon the lowly beast of burden but upon the horse of war. "And I saw heaven opened, and behold a white horse; and he that sat upon him was called Faithful and True, and in righteousness he doth judge and make war. . . . And he hath on his vesture and on his thigh a name written, KING OF KINGS, AND LORD OF LORDS" (Rev. 19:11, 16). What a triumphal entry that will be! From Armageddon the King will move on in triumph until He establishes again the throne of David and reigns over the whole earth.

Many books and pamphlets have been published in recent years setting forth the plain Scriptural predictions and promises, which cannot be broken, of the Lord's personal, visible, bodily return to earth. One among many such passages may be mentioned here to remind us of something that we might forget, and that is, that the indwelling of the Holy Spirit in every believer is a promise of the Second Coming of Christ. "The presence of the Third Person of the Holy Trinity is a proof, a pledge, a promise, and secures the return sooner or later of the Second Person." For Paul writes to those who have "first trusted in Christ," that "after that ye believed, ye were sealed with that holy Spirit of promise, which is the earnest of our inheritance until the redemption of the purchased possession" (Eph. 1:13, 14). Christ has already bought us with His blood, but He has not yet fully redeemed His purchased possession. So "ourselves also, which have the firstfruits of the Spirit, even we ourselves groan within ourselves, waiting for the adoption, to wit, the redemption of our body. For we are saved by hope" (Rom. 8:23, 24). And that hope, which is a God-covenanted certainty, is the Lord's return.

III

IS THE ADVENT HOPE PRACTICAL?

BELIEF in the Second Coming of Christ is *the only practical way to make our Christian life and activity worth while.* There are many true Christians who do not realize this, and whose activities therefore are directed in impractical and useless channels.

I remember, not long before the World War broke in 1914, talking with three intimate friends about the Lord's return.

One was a business man of large means and responsibilities, who was known the world around for his Sunday school leadership, and who was also deeply concerned for true soul winning. I asked him whether he had ever specially studied the subject of the Lord's return. "No," he replied with a friendly smile. "I have had to be a practical man all my life, a business man, and I have never had time to look much into that subject." Later I was with this Sunday school leader and a group of friends, while attending the World's Sunday School Convention in Zurich, Switzerland, and the subject of the Lord's return was mentioned. "You do not think," said he, "that the Lord will come back until we have made this world a fit place for Him to come to, do you?"

Another of the three was a lawyer, an earnest Christian and an elder in the church I then attended. When I asked him the same question, he answered: "I have never been specially interested in speculative matters of that sort."

The third was a devoted Christian woman and mother, active in the Sunday school and church; and she answered: "All I am interested in is doing the Lord's work, and then, no matter when He may or may not come, it is all the same with me. I am only interested in doing what He has given me to do."

These three typical Christians, the business man, the

lawyer, and the mother and Sunday school teacher, did not realize that they were all impractical in their hopes and purposes in Christian activity, while priding themselves on being practical. Indeed, when the World War broke, the business man frankly admitted that his Christian faith was almost shattered. He had supposed that Christianity was so far on its way toward converting the world that there never could be another great war. Those who were intelligently clear on the Bible's teaching, that wars must continue until the Lord comes again, were not surprised by the cataclysm that broke in 1914. Is it practical to be so ignorant of a great, dominant teaching of the Bible that one almost loses faith when plainly predicted events come to pass?

As for the Christian lawyer's thought that the Lord's return is a "speculative matter," if that is so, then the Gospel also is "speculative," and we are left in uncertainty whether Christ really died for our sins, and whether He can save those who trust Him as Saviour. For the Gospel of salvation and the Second Coming of Christ rest on one and the same foundation—the Word of God. And—God be praised!—the inspired and infallible Word is never speculative, but "all the promises of God in him [Christ] are yea, and in him Amen" (2 Cor. 1:20).

There are many Christian activities today which, while carried on by those who are really Christians, are yet utterly futile and hopeless in God's sight. For they are directed toward ushering in world-wide peace, toward "Christianizing the social order," and toward other ends that are hopeless until "that blessed hope" has been fulfilled by the return of Christ Himself, Who alone can do certain things that He has never asked His Church to do in this present age.

The late Edward Bok was a man of remarkable ability, of wide knowledge, and of genuine altrusim—but he did some things he would never have done had he known the truth of the Lord's return. For example, he offered a prize of $100,000 for the best plan for world peace. There were upwards of 22,000 applicants for this prize, and it was awarded to one of these for an elaborate peace plan which, needless to say, has not yet worked out.

For a Christian to be ignorant of the Second Coming of Christ, and of the course of this age, and of the true mission of the Church,—which is not to convert the world but to evangelize the world,—is to be like mariners sailing an ocean without chart or compass; like travelers setting out to reach a certain destination but moving steadily in a wrong direction. It is not practical to attempt to do what God does not want us to do, and what He says we cannot do. If we would be really practical, we must know what the Lord meant when He said, "Occupy till I come" (Luke 19:13).

King George V of England, ruler over the Empire "on which the sun never sets," was a Christian monarch, trusted and beloved throughout the world. But apparently he did not know as much of the truth of the Second Coming as did his godly grandmother, Queen Victoria. In June, 1933, he opened the World Economic Conference in London with the words: "I believe this to be the first time in history that any Sovereign has presided at the opening of a conference of all the nations of all the world." Then in an address partly in French and partly in English he continued:

> The world is in its unquiet state, and for you gentlemen, who from today begin the work of restoration, the task is heavy. It will not be achieved except through good will and sincere co-operation. . . . I fully recognize the magnitude of the tasks of this conference, but there is evidence of a real desire to reach agreement which gives me hope. All nations are suffering from a common ill. . . . In the face of a crisis which all realize and acknowledge, I appeal to you all to co-operate for the sake of the ultimate good of the whole world. It cannot be beyond the powers of man so to use the vast resources of the world as to assure the material progress of civilization. . . . Now is the opportunity to harness this new consciousness of common interests to the service of mankind.

Surely this, with many other governmental expressions of hope for world-wide agreement and peace, is a pathetic evidence of the ignorance of men and the futility of their efforts. There was no mention of God or of the Lord Jesus Christ in this inaugural from a Christian monarch; nor has God been recognized in recent international declarations, whether at Geneva, Locarno, London, or Washington. But a time is coming when the King shall come Who alone can heal "all nations suffering from a common ill"; for God has promised, when that time comes, "that at the name of Jesus every knee should bow, of things in heaven, and things in earth, and things under the earth; and that every tongue should confess that Jesus Christ is Lord, to the glory of God the Father" (Phil. 2: 10, 11).

It is sometimes said, by those who are ignorant of the Bible's teaching concerning our Lord's return and of Christian history and present-day facts, that belief in the Second Coming of Christ "cuts the nerve of foreign missions" and deadens the Christian's sense of responsibility, even paralyzing Christian activity. But to expect the return of a loved one does not deaden our energy. It does not paralyze our activities. On the contrary, if we know that a dearly loved member of the family who has been away on a journey is to come back today, are we not likely to exert ourselves to be ready, that we may give the best kind of welcome? So it is for the Christian who is eagerly looking for the Lord's return.

It does not paralyze Christian activity, though some who do not understand this Bible truth mistakenly think it does. A medical missionary has written me from Korea:

Some time ago a fine, spiritual Bible woman took dinner with us. She spends a great deal of time in prayer and in doing evangelistic work. Those who think that the doctrine of the Lord's return is crippling to evangelistic work—I would like to have had heard a remark of hers. Some of her relatives—her own family, I believe—are not Christians. They live a long distance from here. She said she thought the Lord would be coming soon, and that some of her own folks were not saved, and so she was going to take this long trip to see them and try to lead them to him.

It is a "blessed hope" indeed that energizes the child of God to win to Christ all that can be reached before His coming. And we find that the New Covenant, the New Testament, of our Lord Jesus Christ, sets forth the hope of His return as one of the greatest incentives to good works in His name.

IV

OTHER REASONS FOR THE BLESSED HOPE

ANOTHER reason for believing in the Second Coming of Christ is found in *the many predicted signs* of the end of the age and of His personal, visible, bodily return. The most of these signs, plainly predicted both by the Lord Himself and also by the divinely inspired prophets of the Old Testament and of the New, show the steadily increasing downhill course of this age and the progressive deterioration both of the world and of the professing Christian Church.

Scriptural prophecy deals a deathblow to both of those strange and unscriptural theories known as postmillennialism and amillennialism.

The Scripturally predicted signs of the end of the age, picturing conditions prevailing in the world and in the professing Church just before the Lord's return, give no foundation for the popular but mistaken hope that the world is growing better and that humanity is steadily and successfully climbing up hill. This is the falsely optimistic hope of the postmillennialist, who believes that the Church will eventually win the whole world to Christ and righteousness and thus bring in the millennium, after which will come the return of the Lord and "the end of the world."

The word "postmillennial" means, of course, "after the millennium"; that is, that the Lord will return only after the millennium, or Golden Age, has been established on earth.

The word "amillennial," on the other hand, means "without a millennium," or "non-millennial." Those holding this view, while they believe in the Lord's return, strangely fail to see in the Scriptures the many plain predictions of a glorious future for God's chosen people Israel here on earth, and the earthly millennium, or Golden Age, which the

Scriptures tell us can come only when Christ comes again, and will come as surely as "all the promises of God in him [Christ] are yea, and in him Amen" (2 Cor. 1:20).

In distinction from, and in rejection of, both the post-millennial and the amillennial theories, is the view known as "premillennialism," meaning "before the millennium,"—that is, that Christ will come before (and bring by His coming) the thousand years of righteousness on earth. This view is held by most of the outstanding evangelical Bible teachers, evangelists, and missionaries of our generation and by many of the past half-century or more, in which time there has been such a notable revival of study and acceptance of the truth of the Lord's return and the whole body of prophetic Scriptures.

The predicted signs of the Second Coming of Christ are taken up fully in later chapters. The questions are faced and discussed: Are there really signs showing that the Lord's return is near, and, if so, have we any right to believe that we can interpret such signs safely?

Still another reason for believing in the Lord's return is because, according to God's Word, *only thus can God's promises to Israel be fulfilled*. The Old Testament is filled with promises of Israel's lasting glory as a nation on earth. Those promises have never yet been kept—but God always keeps His word. They were not kept in Old Testament times, for Israel went down into humiliating captivity. They certainly were not kept when Christ came to earth in His incarnation, for Israel rejected Him. The promise to Mary, before the birth of the babe Jesus, that "the Lord God shall give unto him the throne of his father David: and he shall reign over the house of Jacob for ever; and of his kingdom there shall be no end" (Luke 1:32-34), has not yet been kept.

But it must be, and will be. The throne of David is still empty—but it shall be occupied, here on earth, by David's Greater Son. Paul the true Israelite writes by inspiration:

I say then, Hath God cast away his people? God forbid. . . . And so all Israel shall be saved: as it is written, There shall come out of Sion the Deliverer, and shall turn away ungodliness from Jacob: for this is my covenant unto them, when I shall take away their sins (Rom. 11:1-27).

There is a magnificent future ahead for God's chosen people Israel. This is taken up in a later chapter. As John Wilkerson has said:

The Church is the Gospel express train, stopping at a few stations to pick up a few passengers, the train "Israel" being side-tracked to let the express go by. When Christ comes, the train "Israel" will be switched back upon the main line, stop at all stations, and take on the world.

We should believe in the Second Coming of Christ *because it is a purifying hope*. "Beloved, now are we the sons of God, and it doth not yet appear what we shall be: but we know that, when he shall appear, we shall be like him; for we shall see him as he is. And every man that hath this hope in him purifieth himself, even as he is pure" (1 John 3:2, 3).

The late Dr. John Roach Straton, valiant defender of the faith, gave this testimony:

I wish to bear my own personal testimony that I did not overcome the habit of smoking until the truth of the return of our Lord came home clearly to my mind and heart. When I did thus believe that Jesus Christ is surely coming back to this world again, even as He plainly promised, and that His coming for His church—the redeemed—may be at any moment, I found grace to throw pipes and cigars away completely never to take them up again. I did not want Jesus to come back and find me with a breath that was offensive, or presenting the sorry spectacle of a preacher with a pipe or cigar in the corner of his mouth!

Howard A. Banks used to tell of a personal friend of his in the South, many years ago, who had been a man of the world, then was saved and instructed under the preaching and teaching of Dr. James H. Brookes. He had been in the habit of stopping at a saloon, at his noontime lunch hour, and getting a glass of beer—he had not questioned this, before his conversion, any more than he would have questioned drinking a glass of milk. But one day, after he had gone into the saloon and ordered his beer, the thought came to him: "Suppose the Lord should come at this moment!" He had lifted the glass from the bar, but before it reached his lips he set it down again, paid for it, turned on his heel and left the saloon, and never again did he enter a saloon except to try to win some one to Christ. For him, as for Dr. Straton, the blessed hope was purifying.

We should believe in the Second Coming *because it is the only hope there is in the world today*. It is a hopeless world we are looking out upon if we fix our eyes upon men, upon governments, upon even the professing Christian Church, in which apostasy has made such tragic and increasing inroads. There is no hope on any earth level. But as we join the disciples in "gazing up into heaven," we see a hope that is hope indeed! It can no more fail than God can fail. It is no mirage or will-o'-the-wisp, as men's plans are. It is "that blessed hope, and the glorious appearing of the great God and our Saviour Jesus Christ."

As the late Bishop J. C. Ryle said truly:

I believe it is for the safety, comfort, and happiness of all true Christians to expect as little as possible from churches or governments under the present dispensation; to hold themselves ready for tremendous convulsions and changes of all things established; and so to expect their good things only from Christ's Second Advent.

As Israel's faithful souls were comforted by prophecies of the first advent of Christ, so we now need the consolations of the lamp of prophecy in this time of spiritual darkness. And surely it cannot be long, now, until the "great voices" shall begin to sound in Heaven, saying, "The kingdoms of this world are become the kingdoms of our Lord, and of his Christ; and he shall reign for ever and ever" (Rev. 11:15).

And finally, we believe in the Second Coming of Christ because we find here *a comfort that can be found nowhere else*. Death brings heartbreak and sorrow, even among God's people. Death is an enemy, not a friend. As we grow older, more and more of our loved ones are taken from us to be with the Lord. The separation sometimes seems more than we can bear. But there comes this wonderful word:

But I would not have you to be ignorant, brethren, concerning them which are asleep, that ye sorrow not, even as others which have no hope. For if we believe that Jesus died and rose again, even so them also which sleep in Jesus will God bring with him. For this we say unto you by the word of the Lord, that we which are alive and remain unto the coming of the Lord shall not prevent [precede] them which are asleep. For the Lord himself shall descend from heaven with a shout, with the voice of the archangel, and with the trump of God: and the dead in Christ shall rise first: then we which are alive and remain shall be caught up together with them in the clouds, to meet the Lord in the air: and so shall we ever be with the Lord. Wherefore comfort one another with these words (1 Thess. 4:13-18).

V

HOW I CAME TO BELIEVE IT

IT SEEMS strange that so many Christian people who are rejoicing today in "that blessed hope" of the Lord's personal, visible, bodily return to establish His Kingdom on earth and bring in the millennium of His personal reign, should have lived many years as sincere Christians, without believing this precious truth or even knowing much about it. Yet such is the fact, and the past quarter of a century has witnessed many testimonies of this sort from God's people. "Once we were blind, but now we see."

The Sunday School Times has published a number of testimonies on "How I Came to Believe in Our Lord's Return," including the personal experiences of such Christian leaders as Drs. James M. Gray, A. C. Gaebelein, W. B. Riley, Lewis Sperry Chafer, William L. Pettingill, Mark A. Matthews, Canon F. E. Howitt, and others.[1]

In my undergraduate days at Yale University I studied the Bible as a freshman under that scholarly and magnetic Higher Critic, Professor William R. Harper, later President of the University of Chicago, and in junior and senior years I elected courses in Bible study under similar "modern" and critical teaching. In the years that followed my graduation, and in my early editorial work, I was firmly convinced that the world was steadily growing better, and I thought of "premillenarians" as mistaken but harmless cranks, though I had no intelligent understanding of their position and teaching.

I had the unspeakable blessing of early home training in

---

[1] These have been brought together in a booklet, including others on *Why I Believe the Lord's Return is Near,* and published by The Bible Institute Colportage Association, 843 North Wells Street, Chicago; 5 cents each, 40 cents a dozen, $2.75 a hundred.

a Christian family and under Christian parents to whom I owe everything. The observance of the Lord's Day was both strict and beautiful in our home, and I rejoiced in the fact that America was a Christian land and that the notorious "Continental Sabbath" of Europe was not found here.

Shortly after graduating from Yale I made my first trip abroad, with my beloved father, H. Clay Trumbull. We were in Germany and France first, and I remember being impressed and shocked by the wide open, godless Sundays there, especially in Paris, where the Lord's Day was not a holy day but a holiday of unrestricted amusement and pleasure-seeking. Then we crossed the Channel to England, and I remember my first Sunday in London, where life on that Lord's Day was almost as quiet as in a New England village. I contrasted Christian Britain's Sunday with that of the godless Continent, and I rejoiced that this honoring of God's Day was a bulwark of the Christian civilization of Great Britain and America.

But I had begun to be disturbed, even before that first trip abroad, as I had traveled in some of our midwest states and noticed that Sunday was more "wide open" than in the eastern states; theaters were beginning to be opened on Sundays, and other intimations of the "Continental Sabbath" were appearing.

As the years passed I could not but observe an increase of worldliness and the breakdown of the sacredness of the Lord's Day. But I bolstered up my conviction and faith that the world was nevertheless growing better, as best I could. For surely Christianity must prevail in the long run.

I read a series of magazine articles in which a well known writer took up church conditions and spiritual life. He claimed that church conditions were very lamentable, that religious life was declining rather than improving. He gave what purported to be facts; but I said to myself: "It's 'up to me' to show how mistaken this man is. I must do it some time. The Church is all right. Christianity is going to prevail." I confess that I dreaded getting into the subject, because I did not quite know how I was going to get out. I could not see clearly how I was going to prove that this writer was in the wrong, though I felt sure he was.

I read also another magazine article, entitled "Blasting at the Rock of Ages," in which the writer endeavored to show that in our colleges many professors were sowing seeds of unbelief. He took his proof right from the lips of the professors themselves. He made out a pretty good case; but I said to myself: "This is all nonsense. He has just taken a few detached sentences, not representative of the men who spoke them and not representative of our educational institutions. I shall be able to clear this up some time."

One day one of the workers in *The Sunday School Times* office made the suggestion: "Would it not be well to take up in our paper a live topic that would interest every one, such as child labor and factory conditions? Here is a big problem which is certainly the business of a religious paper, and of the Church of Christ." I said I would think about it. I rather shrank from entering upon it; yet was it not the duty of the Church to solve such problems?

So I went on, facing these actual, not imaginary problems, which current literature and everyday events were bringing before me.

The years passed on, and there came a spiritual crisis in my life. Through the deepest, most convicting sense of personal spiritual need, and after prolonged prayer for God's deliverance and a new empowering for everyday living as well as for Christian service, God in His infinite patience and grace met my need by showing me the Scriptural truth of union with Christ and the indwelling Christ.[2]

Not long after, as I was visiting in the home of my friends Dr. and Mrs. Robert E. Speer, I was telling Mrs. Speer's mother (Mrs. Bailey, of Harrisburg) something of what the Lord had done for me in such a gracious and revolutionizing way. When I had finished, Mrs. Bailey said quietly: "Mr. Trumbull, have you ever specially studied the subject of the Second Coming of Christ?"

[2] Details of this experience and new realization of Christ's indwelling as the Christian's life are given in the pamphlet, *The Life That Wins*, which may be had from The Sunday School Times Company at 2 cents each, 20 cents a dozen, $1.50 per hundred, postpaid.

"No," I said, "I have not."

"Do so," she replied earnestly, "and do so at once; it is the key to the Bible."

I had never heard anyone speak in just that way before. I assured Mrs. Bailey that I should be glad to do as she said, and I asked her how I could go about it. "Are there any books on the subject?" I asked.

"Oh, yes," she replied, "there are books you can easily get," and she mentioned one, *Jesus is Coming*, by W. E. B.[3] I began reading that book and others that I was surprised to find were easily obtainable. I might add that, some years later, I had the great privilege of meeting Mr. Blackstone, author of the precious book *Jesus is Coming,* which has been used of God to revolutionize Bible study, the ministry, and personal lives of countless Christians. As I sat next to him one evening at the supper table in the home of the Christian and Missionary Alliance in Philadelphia, Mr. Blackstone told me how he came to write his book. He had felt the need of such a book, and he did everything in his power to get other men who, he felt, were much better able to write it than he, to undertake the work. He could not persuade them to do so, but they persuaded him to do it, and his book has circled the globe in many different languages, bringing blessings to countless lives.

I was telling my beloved friend, the late Dr. James M. Gray, how the Lord had shown me the truth of His return after I had seen the truth of union with Christ. "When a Christian discovers the indwelling Christ," said Dr. Gray, "he soon begins to look for the returning Christ."

There were other vital factors that God used to open my blind eyes to the truth of the Lord's return. It was about the same time, I remember, that I had the privilege of a conversation with that great evangelist and Bible teacher, Dr. George F. Pentecost. We were talking about the question of the Church of Christ converting or Christianizing the world, and Dr. Pentecost startled me as he pointed out that heathendom was gaining on Christendom at the rate (I think he said) of about a thousand to one every year.

[3] Revell Company, 50 cents paper, 75 cents cloth.

At that rate, he asked me, just when would the Church convert the world?

I shall never forget an all-day train ride I had with Dr. Robert McWatty Russell, then President of Westminster College, at New Wilmington, Pennsylvania, later a member of the staff of Moody Bible Institute. We were chatting together, and Dr. Russell asked me what I knew of Kingdom truth; he called it, I think, "the lost Kingdom view of the Church." I knew nothing about it; I did not even know what he was talking about, and I lost no time in saying so.

Then Dr. Russell began to explain to me what he meant. He opened up the Scriptures to me in a way that I had never heard before. I listened to this gifted, consecrated, and eloquent Bible teacher as he held me spellbound, almost breathless with interest and excitement, over the marvelous panorama that he spread before me. I am inclined to think, although that was some twenty-five years ago and I made no notes on our conversation, that "beginning at Moses and all the prophets, he expounded unto them [me] in all the Scriptures the things concerning" the Lord's return and the millennial Kingdom on earth.

"Oh, Dr. Russell," I exclaimed, "you must write an article on this for *The Sunday School Times*." I think he said he would, but somehow it was never written. But, God be praised, the Lord Himself took charge of *The Sunday School Times* in such matters, and He began to set forth in its pages the Kingdom truth of the Lord's return, the blessed hope of the Church, and Israel's glorious future on earth.

As I read the books of Bible teachers who shared with their readers the joy of the Lord's return, and then as I "searched the scriptures daily, whether those thing were so" (Acts 17:11), I found the Second Coming of Christ blazing forth in glory from almost every page of the Bible! I had seen the Scofield Reference Bible before this, but had paid no attention to it. Now I secured a copy, and never can I forget the thrilling joy that came into my life as I used it in my daily devotional Bible reading, and studied the notes and comments and chain references, and began to enter into the riches that Dr. Scofield had brought together through thirty years of his own Bible study and from the treasure houses of the greatest Bible students and scholars of half a century.

Yes, Mrs. Bailey was right. The Second Coming of Christ is the key that unlocks the Bible. Bible passages I had never been able to understand, which had seemed dark and incomprehensible, shone forth in their real meaning when once I had accepted God's Word about the return of His Son to this earth to do what the Church never can do and never has been commissioned to do. As Augustine said: "Distinguish the ages, and the Scriptures harmonize." The Scofield Reference Bible opened my blind eyes to the ages or dispensations, which God has ordained as periods of time during which He has made, and will yet make, specific tests of man.

One closing word in this personal testimony. As one and another of the members of the staff of *The Sunday School Times* came to see and rejoice in the truths of the indwelling Christ as our life and victory, and of the sure and covenanted return of Christ, we began to bring these truths into the columns of the paper for which we were responsible. We could not but share with others the blessings that God was so graciously giving us. A dear friend and counselor of mine at that time, as he has continued to be through the years, Dr. Henry W. Frost of the China Inland Mission, said one day to his warm friend and counselor, the late Dr. William J. Erdman, "Mr. Trumbull is bringing the truth of the Second Coming of Christ into *The Sunday School Times.*"

"Has he counted the cost?" Dr. Erdman asked. Dr. Frost told me of this conversation, and passed the question on to me.

No, I had not counted the cost. The question came as a genuine surprise, for it had never occurred to me to think of "counting the cost" of sharing such rich and abounding blessings as were now filling my own life and the lives of other loved ones of the staff and in our family circle and among our friends. Dr. Erdman meant, of course, that the truth of the Lord's return was not a "popular" one in certain theological circles and among many ministers and churches,—it has vastly increased its hold upon ministers and churches and Christian people in the quarter of a century since then.

But there was a "cost," and this is what it was. During the next few years after we began sharing with readers of *The Sunday School Times* the Scriptural truths concerning the indwelling Christ, union with Christ, and the blessed hope of the Lord's return to establish His Kingdom on earth, the circulation of the paper increased by some thirty thousand copies a week and The Sunday School Times Company began, for the first time since its incorporation a dozen years earlier, to pay dividends to the little group of Christian stockholders, whose support and co-operation had been vital factors in the life and ministry of the paper.

Is it not always true that, when we do God's will and declare the whole counsel of God, we can safely look to Him to take care of the "cost"?

VI

PROPHECY'S GREATEST MIRACLE

WHO is the greatest man living today? The question would get different answers in different countries. Ask it in Russia, and the answer would be quick and positive—certainly if there were any listeners: "Comrade Stalin." Ask it in Italy, and no one would dare voice any reply but "Il Duce," Mussolini. In Germany the question would meet with an instant "Der Fuehrer," Hitler. In such Christian lands as Great Britain, Canada, and the United States the replies would be many and varied, and with frank recognition that only uncertain opinion could be ventured.

But there is an answer to the question, different from that given by admirers of the great Dictators and wholly removed from the uncertainties of human opinion. God has given us his own answer, undebatable and final.

The greatest man living today is the Lord Jesus Christ.

Do we not often forget that the risen, ascended, and glorified Son of God is also a Man? This realization came to me in a new way, a few years ago, as I picked up a tract by Norman H. Camp entitled, "The Greatest Man Living Today." It bore the subtitle, "Who is He? Where is He?" The first paragraph read:

If some one in whom you had confidence should tell you that a man—a remarkable man—is living today in a material body of flesh and bones, and is now over nineteen hundred years old, would you believe it? If you were convinced that this man—this remarkable man—is really living and that you would some day see him face to face, and be judged by him for all the deeds you have ever done or ever will do, what would you think?

The tract went on to say:

43

Methuselah lived to the remarkable age of nine hundred and sixty-nine years, but he is not living today in a body of flesh and bones. There is only one Man, out of all the millions of men who have lived and died, whose body was raised from the grave, —"never to see corruption," and who today is living in that same body and flesh and bones which he received at the time of his miraculous birth and who will live in that body forever. Death can never touch him again. . . . He is seated on the right hand of the Majesty on High. He has all power in Heaven and on earth. His name is Jesus! [1]

Divine prophecy predicted that Christ, after He had died by crucifixion, should rise again from the dead, and it predicted that this Greatest Man Living Today shall come back again to this earth to reign, not only as a Dictator but as "King of kings, and Lord of lords."

Prophecy's greatest miracle is resurrection—the resurrection of Christ, the resurrection of all the dead, both saved and lost.

Resurrection is a central, dominant theme of Bible prophecy, running through the Scriptures, both Old Testament and New. Resurrection, or the restoring of life to the dead, is a miracle. A miracle is something that only God can do, working not by any natural law but by His own sovereign power. Some scientists and physicians would have us believe that eventually man will discover the secret of life and be able to conquer death. A popular book on the remarkable achievements made by science in coping with disease is entitled *Men Against Death,* and the publishers' announcement said, "Life stuff is believed to be potentially immortal." They overlook the fact that all "life stuff" on earth today is poisoned by sin, and that "the wages of sin is death." "Men against death" are doomed to failure; only God can deal with death, and he does so only through his Son, Jesus Christ.

A secular magazine of enormous circulation recently published an article under the title, "Is It Right to Bring Back the Dead?" It was written by a well known New York physician, who said: "There is little doubt in my mind

---

[1] The tract, *The Greatest Man Living Today,* may be ordered from the Bible Institute Colportage Association, 843 N. Wells Street, Chicago; 3 cents each, 30 cents a dozen, $2 a hundred.

that this year or next, or in ten or in twenty or in fifty years, it will be no more difficult for medical men to bring back to life a human being killed by accident or disease than it is now to administer a hypodermic to restore a patient's faculties after a prolonged spell of fainting." He cited cases where a man and a dog, apparently dead, had been restored to life. He went on to say: "But there is a serious question as to whether the law of the land sanctions the duplication by science of Biblical miracles."

The entire article is a startling evidence of the blindness of the natural man to facts so plain and undeniable that it seems impossible that intelligent human beings can miss them. Dead men will never be restored to life by science. Biblical miracles will never be duplicated by science. The law of the land need not worry as to how to meet this situation—it will never arise.

But dead men are going to be brought back to life—perhaps this year or the next, and certainly at some time. God declares this, and his prophecies never fail.

It is important to be sure that we understand the meaning of the word resurrection as used in God's Word. It never means merely continued spiritual existence, as many Modernists say, but in most Bible passages it means the restoring of the dead *body* to life. A missionary to Japan told me, years ago, of a conversation he had with a theological professor who had said to him in conversation, "I believe in the resurrection of Jesus."

The missionary asked: "What do you mean by the resurrection of Jesus? Do you mean that His physical body was raised from the grave?"

With a sneer the theological professor answered: "No, of course I don't believe that. I believe His body decomposed and went back to the ground like every other human body. But I believe the soul of Jesus rose from the dead and is permeating human society today." So this teacher of young ministers believed that Christians could sing of the resurrection of the Son of God and Saviour of sinners only a paraphrase of the old song, "John Brown's body lies a-mouldering in the grave, his soul goes marching on."

But resurrection is not only a miracle, and a dominant

theme of Bible prophecy; it is prophecy's greatest miracle. There can be no doubt of this as we read the Scriptures.

Death is Satan's worst. Resurrection is God's best. Sin is the worst thing that can come to man—and it comes to all men. For "by one man sin entered into the world, and death by sin; and so death passed upon all men, for that all have sinned" (Rom. 5:12). And not only is death the wages of sin (Rom. 6:23), but Satan, man's worst enemy along with sin, has been given the power of death (Heb. 2:14).

What was Christ's supreme mission in leaving Heaven and becoming man? The whole Bible answers—it was to save lost sinners, redeeming them from the power of sin and death. He came "to give his life a ransom for many" (Matt. 20:28). He took upon Himself flesh and blood in order that He might die, and He died "that through death he might destroy him that had the power of death, that is, the devil; and deliver them who through fear of death were all their lifetime subject to bondage" (Heb. 2:14, 15). "For this purpose the Son of God was manifested, that he might destroy the works of the devil" (1 John 3:8),—and the worst of those works are sin and death.

Therefore God's greatest miracle, His supreme miracle, is that victory over death which consists of resurrection—the resurrection of the body as well as of the soul and spirit that are "dead in trespasses and sins" (Eph. 2:1).

The resurrection of the body of the believer is an imperative necessity if God is to be true to His trust—and He is! He asks us to give Him our bodies. "I beseech you therefore, brethren, by the mercies of God, that ye present your bodies a living sacrifice" (Rom. 12:1). After we have done this, and—should the Lord not come before we die— have then gone down into death trusting in God's Son as our Saviour, and our bodies have had to succumb to the power of death and the ravages of physical corruption, is God going to abandon that which we have given Him, leaving it for all eternity in the power of the enemy, death? God forbid! We know that these bodies shall be raised from the dead, for, with Paul, "I know whom I have believed, and am persuaded that he is able to keep that which I have committed unto him against that day" (2 Tim. 1:12). "For our conversation [citizenship] is in heaven; from whence also we look for the Saviour, the Lord Jesus Christ: who shall change our vile body [body of humiliation] that it may be fashioned like unto his glorious body [body of glory] according to the working whereby he is able even to subdue all things unto himself" (Phil. 3:20, 21).

There are many other Scriptures that show that the resurrection of the body is God's greatest miracle. One of the most convincing is given in Paul's inspired prayer in Ephesians 1:15-23. The apostle prays that the eyes of the understanding of all children of God may be enlightened, that they may know their hope and their riches, "and what is the exceeding greatness of his power to us-ward who believe, *according to the working of his mighty power, which he wrought in Christ, when he raised him from the dead, and set him at his own right hand in the heavenly places, far above all principality, and power, and might, and dominion, and every name that is named, not only in this world, but also in that which is to come: and hath put all things under his feet.*" As some one has said, God was able to take a dead man and make him Business Manager of the universe.

Death is never a friend, always an enemy; and there can be no unconquered enemies of God and Christ and His children in eternity—if there were such an enemy it would be a lasting reproach to, and reflection upon, the power of Christ. So we read in the great resurrection chapter, 1 Corinthians 15, that Christ "must reign, till he hath put all enemies under his feet. The last enemy that shall be destroyed is death." And death can be done away and destroyed only by releasing from its power those over whom it was allowed for a time to operate. So the resurrection of the body is Christ's supreme triumph and prophecy's greatest miracle.

A California pastor, with whom I have had precious fellowship in prayer and conference ministry on the Pacific Coast, wrote in a personal letter a few years ago:

On Easter morning I was enabled to give a message on Revelation 1:18: "I am he that liveth, and was dead; and, behold, I am alive for evermore." Never before had I seen so clearly, nor been permitted to bring others so clearly, the fact that in celebrating the resurrection of our Lord we are celebrating the greatest victory ever won.

In what some Bible scholars believe to have been the first book of the Bible that was written, Job, is one of the most glorious prophecies of the resurrection of the body. In the agony, almost despair, of his physical and spiritual suffering, tempted by his own wife to "curse God, and die," Job's faith cries out: "I know that my redeemer liveth, and that he shall stand at the latter day upon the earth: and though after my skin worms destroy this body, yet in my flesh shall I see God: whom I shall see for myself, and mine eyes shall behold, and not another; though my reins be consumed within me" (Job 19:25-27).

Daniel, the great prophet of the end of the age in which we are now living, whose inspired writing was quoted by the Lord Jesus as an authority (Matt. 24:15), was enabled by inspiration to predict that in a far distant future "many of them that sleep in the dust of the earth shall awake, some to everlasting life, and some to shame and everlasting contempt" (Dan. 12:2).

So Daniel predicts the two resurrections, those of the saved and of the lost, declared by the Lord both in His earthly lifetime and in the Revelation. To the Jews, Christ gave the Gospel invitation and at the same time the solemn warning of prophecy:

Verily, verily, I say unto you, The hour is coming, and now is, when the dead shall hear the voice of the Son of God: and they that hear shall live. . . . Marvel not at this: for the hour is coming, in the which all that are in the graves shall hear his voice, and shall come forth; they that have done good, unto the resurrection of life; and they that have done evil, unto the resurrection of damnation (John 5:25, 28, 29).

Those who mistakenly think that the Scriptures teach only a "general resurrection" in which, at one and the same time, all men shall be raised from the dead (both the saved and the lost), ignore the inspired teaching "that no prophecy of the scripture is of any private [that is, isolated or detached] interpretation" (2 Pet. 1:20), and they fail to read Daniel and John in the light of the Lord's prophecy in Revelation, where John was shown risen saints who "lived and reigned with Christ a thousand years," and then at once was told that "the rest of the dead lived not again until the thousand years were finished." We have the divine explanation concerning those who lived and reigned with Christ:

This is the first resurrection. Blessed and holy is he that hath part in the first resurrection: on such the second death hath no power, but they shall be priests of God and of Christ, and shall reign with him a thousand years (Rev. 20:4-6).

The resurrection of those who reject Christ is predicted as coming a thousand years later, when John saw

The dead, small and great, stand before God. . . . And the sea gave up the dead which were in it; and death and hell [hades] delivered up the dead which were in them: and they were judged every man according to their works. And death and hell [hades] were cast into the lake of fire. This is the second death. And whosoever was not found written in the book of life was cast into the lake of fire (Rev. 20:11-15).

It is a solemn, awe-inspiring thought, that God's power is so great that He can bring to life the dead bodies even of lost souls. So prophecy's greatest miracle is manifested in the resurrection of the lost as well as of the saved. But its supreme triumph is in doing away with all the effects and consequences of sin, including the death of the body, for those who have received the Son of God as their Saviour. To them comes the glad assurance:

So when this corruptible shall have put on incorruption, and this mortal shall have put on immortality, then shall be brought to pass the saying that is written, Death is swallowed up in victory. O death, where is thy sting? O grave, where is thy victory? The sting of death is sin; and the strength of sin is the law. But thanks be to God, which giveth us the victory through our Lord Jesus Christ (1 Cor. 15:54-57).

Prophecy assures the Lord's return, and the Lord's return assures the resurrection of the body for all believers who shall have died before His coming, and the instant change into glorified bodies for all who are living when he comes. James H. McConkey has well said:

We know of no event between us and the coming of the Lord. It may be years from now; it may be tomorrow; it may be today. Each generation stands in eager expectancy as on the *very brink of the mightiest miracle of the miracle-working God since the resurrection of His Son from the dead.* The veil of our mortal flesh trembles under the anticipating touch of Him who may at any moment rend it asunder for the outshining of His glory, for the manifestation of the sons of God. This is the climax of this comfort wherewith we are comforted, that the Resurrection may take place at any moment.

The resurrection of the body is prophecy's greatest miracle, climaxing God's grace in salvation and redemption, for it enables those who were "dead in trespasses and sins" to say:

Beloved, now are we the sons of God, and it doth not yet appear what we shall be: but we know that, when he shall appear, we shall be like him; for we shall see him as he is (1 John 3:2).

VII

THREE GREAT PROPHECIES OF THE SHEPHERD PSALMS

HOW much do we know about our salvation? Of one thing we may be sure—there are hidden treasures in it that we have not yet discovered. Perhaps it will take all eternity to find all that God gave us when He saved us. But there is a treasure house of information about our salvation in the Old Testament. We find Christ not only as Israel's Messiah, but also as the Saviour of the world, "in the law of Moses, and in the prophets, and in the psalms." The Old Testament tells us much about our salvation which its writers themselves could not understand:

Of which salvation the prophets have inquired and searched diligently, who prophesied of the grace that should come unto you: searching what, or what manner of time the Spirit of Christ which was in them did signify, when it testified beforehand the sufferings of Christ, and the glory that should follow (1 Pet. 1:10, 11).

It is hoped that this chapter may help to discover some of our unrealized riches in the Psalms.

If you were asked the question, "Which is the Shepherd Psalm?" what would your answer be? "Why, the Twenty-third Psalm, of course!" Suppose some one, hearing the question, should answer, "The Twenty-second Psalm." And suppose some one else answered, "The Twenty-fourth Psalm." Would you be inclined to tell each of these that they were mistaken, and insist on the Twenty-third? Or have you discovered that the Psalms just before and after the one beginning "The Lord is my shepherd" are just as truly Shepherd Psalms?

Each of the three was written by David the shepherd

51

king. Each sets forth a different yet vital work of David's Greater Son, the True Shepherd, of whom all other shepherds, including David himself, are but shadows or types.

There is an infinitely rich, almost endless study in these three Shepherd Psalms. They are at the center of the Bible, and they gather up the heart of the Word in its three great themes. One recalls the incident of a missionary in the mountains of Asia Minor, who had brought together a group of shepherds to read the Bible to them. They were seated around a log fire on a chill night, in a rude cabin. The missionary began reading the tenth chapter of John. As he went on, telling of a sheepfold and sheep and wolf and hireling shepherd and the good shepherd, an eager voice interrupted, "Oh, sir, is that the Gospel?"

"Yes," the missionary replied, "this is the Gospel of Jesus Christ."

"Oh," said the shepherd, his face aglow with pleasure, "I didn't know before that it was a sheep book."

Yes, it is a Book for lost sheep, and it tells of such shepherding as only God's great heart of love could plan and provide.

As prophecy is the heart of the Bible, so these three Psalms gather up and express the heart of God's prophetic Word. The three central prophecies of Scripture are here: the death, the resurrection, and the return of the Son of God, Israel's Messiah, the Saviour of the world, King of kings and Lord of lords.

God's thoughts are not man's thoughts, neither are man's ways God's ways (Isa. 55:8). God's purposes and prophecies cut directly across sinful man's wishes and determination. A German evangelist, Samuel Keller, has brought this out in a striking way. When our Lord hung on the cross, His enemies cried out to him, "Come down and we will believe on you"; but he stayed where He hung and He died there. When He was buried, they sealed the stone and set a watch as though to say, "From now on remain within." But again He did not do what they wished; instead, He arose on the third day. Now that He has passed into the invisible world they cry out, "Remain away! Come not back!" He will not do their pleasure; He is coming again. But in eternity's future there will be a great host of those who were Christ's enemies while He hung on the cross, or while He lay within the tomb, or during the centuries between His ascension and His coming again, who will praise Him because He did not do as they wished.

Our three Shepherd Psalms not only set forth the death, the resurrection, and the return of Christ, they also declare the three tenses of the Gospel of our salvation,—the past, the present, and the future.   Dr. Griffith Thomas used to tell of a beautiful incident that occurred many years ago in the North of England.   A Salvation Army lassie, only recently saved, was overflowing with the joy of the Lord and was eager to share her salvation with all others.   Walking along the street of a little Durham city, she saw a tall, gray-haired man coming toward her and, stranger though he was, she stopped him and said, "Pardon me, sir, but are you saved?"

The tall stranger leaned over toward her and answered, with a quizzical smile playing on his kindly face: "My dear, do you mean *esothen,* or *sozomenos,* or *sothesomai?*"

The Salvation Army lassie was bewildered—it was "all Greek" to her!   She did not know that she had stopped Bishop Westcott, one of the greatest of Greek scholars and an editor of the famous Westcott and Hort edition of the Greek New Testament.   He had asked her, using three different tenses of the Greek verb: "Do you mean, I was saved, or do you mean, I am being saved, or do you mean, I shall be saved?"   And then Bishop Westcott, who was indeed saved and knew that he was saved, lovingly explained a little of the three tenses of the Gospel to the young girl, and showed her something of the riches of her past salvation, her present salvation, and her future salvation; and before they separated that Salvation Army lassie knew more about the Gospel and her Saviour than she had ever known before, and went away rejoicing that she had asked this tall stranger whether he was saved.

The three prophetic Shepherd Psalms give us the past, the present, and the future of the salvation that believers have in Christ.

Many Bible students, including the late Dr. Scofield, have brought out the fact that we have a divine trilogy in the three prophetic Shepherd Psalms.

The three Psalms prophesy, respectively, the mission and work of Christ as the Good Shepherd, the Great Shepherd, and the Chief Shepherd.

Psalm 22. The Good Shepherd.—Written by David more than a thousand years before Christ came, this Psalm is one of the most convincing evidences in the whole Bible of the miraculous and detailed character of inspired prophecy. It could not be understood without the New Testament. It is explained by the words of the Lord in John 10:11: "I am the good shepherd: the good shepherd giveth his life for the sheep." The Lord fulfilled His own prophecy, and David's, when He gave himself up to die on the cross that His sheep might live. And the first words of Psalm 22 are the words that came from our Lord's lips as He hung in agony on the cross, the sinners' Substitute, bearing our sins in His own body on the tree (1 Pet. 2:24): "My God, my God, why hast thou forsaken me?"

The Psalm answers the Saviour's questioning cry. "But thou art holy, O thou that inhabitest the praises of Israel" (v. 3). Our sins were laid upon Christ; He Himself, the Son of God "who knew no sin," was made "to be sin for us" (2 Cor. 5:21). And God cannot look upon sin. For the first time in eternity the Father had to turn His face away from His Son. Christ was forsaken on the cross that we, believing in Him as Saviour, might not be forsaken of God through all eternity.

That is something of what it cost Christ to be the Good Shepherd. A note in the Scofield Reference Bible gathers up other details of the prophecy in this Psalm, describing the death of Christ a thousand years before it occurred:

Psalm 22 is a graphic picture of death by crucifixion. The bones (of the hands, arms, shoulders and pelvis) out of joint (v. 14); the profuse perspiration caused by intense suffering (v. 14); the action of the heart affected (v. 14); strength exhausted, and extreme thirst (v. 15); the hands and feet pierced (v. 16); partial nudity with the hurt to modesty (v. 17), are all incidental to that mode of death. The accompanying circumstances are precisely those fulfilled in the crucifixion of Christ. The desolate cry of verse 1 (Matt. 27: 46); the periods of light and darkness of verse 2 (Matt. 27:45); the contumely of verses 6-8, 12, 13 (Matt. 27:39-43); the casting lots of verse 18

(Matt. 27:35), all were literally fulfilled. When it is remembered that crucifixion was a Roman, not Jewish, form of execution, the proof of inspiration is irresistible.

Dr. A. B. Prichard of Pasadena has called attention to a remarkable fact. The Psalm closes with the statement that "A seed shall serve him," and ends with the words: "They shall come, and shall declare his righteousness unto a people that shall be born, that he hath done this." And the Hebrew translated "he hath done this" is literally, "It is finished," which was one of the last words spoken by the Good Shepherd on the cross.

None but the Good Shepherd has ever laid down His life in this way for his sheep.

Psalm 23. The Great Shepherd.—What Christ did for us on the cross is the past tense of the Gospel and of our salvation. What He is doing for us now, moment by moment, is the present tense; and this most precious of all the Psalms declares it: "The Lord is my shepherd." Only a risen Lord could be our present Saviour. Psalm 22:22 looks forward from crucifixion and death to the resurrection, and Hebrews 13:20, 21 explains the Twenty-third Psalm:

Now the God of peace, that brought again from the dead our Lord Jesus, that great shepherd of the sheep, through the blood of the everlasting covenant, make you perfect in every good work to do his will, working in you that which is well-pleasing in his sight, through Jesus Christ; to whom be glory for ever and ever. Amen.

The Good Shepherd laid down His life for the sheep. But He did so in order that He might take it again (John 10:17). "I have power to lay it down, and I have power to take it again." The Good Shepherd has taken His life again in Psalm 23, having risen from the dead, "that through death he might destroy him that had the power of death, that is, the devil; and deliver them who through fear of death were all their lifetime subject to bondage" (Heb. 2:14, 15). Because a risen Lord is our Great Shepherd, we have nothing to fear! "Yea, though I walk through the valley of the shadow of death, I will fear no evil: for thou art with me."

O death, where is thy sting? O grave, where is thy victory?
The sting of death is sin; and the strength of sin is the law.
But thanks be to God, which giveth us the victory through
our Lord Jesus Christ (1 Cor. 15:55-57).

It is because our Lord died for us, and rose again, and is
living today, and is always with us, that we can KNOW Him.
There is a beautiful incident of a gathering where an aged
minister and a distinguished actor were present. The actor
was asked to give a recitation, and at the minister's request
he repeated the Twenty-third Psalm. It was a very beautiful rendering, and a subdued murmur of praise was heard
when he finished. Then he turned to the old minister and
asked him to repeat the Psalm. When the aged man of
God had finished there were tears in all eyes. And no one
felt the difference more keenly than the great actor. "I
know the Psalm," he said, "but you know the Shepherd."

There are countless incidents showing the blessing of this
wonderful Psalm of David, the shepherd boy, about the
Great Shepherd that was to come from David's line. Just
one other. In a parish church in a small town in Scotland
the evening service was drawing to a close. The pastor had
announced the last hymn, when suddenly the lights went
out. After a moment of silence the precentor rose from his
seat at the front and said: "We cannot manage that hymn,
sir, but we can all sing 'The Lord's My Shepherd' in the
dark."

"Yes, we will take the Twenty-third Psalm," said the
pastor, "and, let me add, it is well with every soul that can
sing, 'The Lord's My Shepherd' *in the dark.*"

The Victorious Life, which is the Gospel in the present
tense for the Christian, is pledged to us in this Psalm. Paul
prays that we may have the eyes of our understanding enlightened and know "what is the exceeding greatness of his
power to us-ward who believe, according to the working of
his mighty power, which he wrought in Christ, when he
raised him from the dead" (Eph. 1:19, 20). We would
have all we need for a life of victory now and here, if we
had only the first half of the first verse of the Twenty-third
Psalm. Mrs. Hannah Whitall Smith, whose book on *The
Christian's Secret of a Happy Life* has brought blessing to

so many, asks God's children to realize that "the Lord is really, and in the very highest sense of the term, a Good Shepherd." Then she suggests repeating the words over and over again, with a different emphasis each time, thus:

The *Lord* is my Shepherd
The Lord *is* my Shepherd.
The Lord is *my* Shepherd.
The Lord is my *Shepherd.*

Psalm 24. The Chief Shepherd.—And now the Shepherd becomes the King of glory! The earth is His, "and the fullness thereof; the world, and they that dwell therein." But this has not yet come to pass—this does not describe conditions today. We are looking for, and awaiting, the future tense of our salvation in the Lord's return, when "the King of glory shall come in." Then indeed: "Lift up your heads, O ye gates; and be ye lift up, ye everlasting doors; and the King of glory shall come in." Do we ask, "Who is this King of glory?" David answers: "The Lord strong and mighty, the Lord mighty in battle. . . . The Lord of hosts, he is the King of glory."

Our Psalm looks forward to a very comforting prophecy given toward the end of the New Testament. Peter exhorts the elders of the churches to "feed the flock of God which is among you"; and by inspiration he promises: "And when the chief Shepherd shall appear, ye shall receive a crown of glory that fadeth not away" (1 Pet. 5:1-5). The sheep that have been saved by the death of the Good Shepherd, have been protected and provided for by the presence of the risen Great Shepherd, shall be rewarded at the coming of the Chief Shepherd.

We think of shepherds as lowly folk—and they are. But God can lift them to the heights. David was a lowly shepherd boy, and God said to him: "I took thee from the sheepcote, even from following the sheep, that thou shouldest be ruler over my people Israel: and I have been with thee . . . and have made thee a name like the name of the great men that are in the earth" (1 Chron. 17:7, 8). It is a remarkable fact that the Greek verb *poimaino,* meaning to feed, to tend a flock, keep sheep, means also to rule, to govern. In 1 Corinthians 9:7 it is used of one who "feedeth a flock."

In John 21:16, the risen Lord commissioned Peter, "Feed my sheep." So in other New Testament passages it is used of shepherding or caring for a flock. But we find the same Greek verb in Matthew 2:6, spoken of Bethlehem: "Out of thee shall come a Governor, that shall rule my people Israel." And in Revelation 12:5 we are told (by the same Greek verb) that Christ shall "rule all nations with a rod of iron."

The Greek noun *poimen*, coming from the verb *poimaino*, means herdsman or shepherd and also manager, director, prince or king. It is the word used of the Good Shepherd in John 10:11; of the Great Shepherd in Hebrews 13:20; and of the Chief Shepherd in 1 Peter 5:4.

So we have one and the same verb or noun for the work of the Good Shepherd, of the Great Shepherd, and of the Chief Shepherd.

In the vision given to John on Patmos, of the "great multitude, which no man could number, of all nations, and kindreds, and people, and tongues," who "stood before the throne, and before the Lamb, clothed with white robes, and palms in their hands," we read that "They shall hunger no more, neither thirst any more." And why? The American Standard Version gives a striking rendering of Revelation 7:17: "For the Lamb that is in the midst of the throne shall be their shepherd, and shall guide them unto fountains of waters of life: and God shall wipe away every tear from their eyes."

A devoted friend of the writer, Joseph Addison Richards, now with the Lord in glory, many years ago wrote a beautiful poem with which this study of the Shepherd Psalms must close:

A Song of the Shepherd

When God sought a king for His people of old,
He went to the fields to find him;
A shepherd was he, with his crook and his lute
And a following flock behind him.

O love of the sheep, O joy of the lute,
And the sling and the stone for the battle!
A shepherd was King; the giant was naught
And the enemy driven like cattle.

When God looked to tell of His good will to men,
And the Shepherd King's Son whom He gave them;
To shepherds, made meek a'caring for sheep,
He told of a Christ sent to save them.

O love of the sheep, O watch in the night,
And the glory, the message, the choir,
'Twas shepherds who saw their King in the straw
And returned with their hearts all on fire.

When Christ thought to tell of His love to the world,
He said to the throng before Him:
"The Good Shepherd giveth His life for the sheep"—
And away to the cross they bore Him.

O love of the sheep, O blood sweat of prayer,
O Man on the cross, God-forsaken!
A Shepherd has gone to defend all alone
The sheepfold by death overtaken.

When God sought a King for His people, for aye,
He went to the grave to find Him;
And a Shepherd came back, Death dead in his grasp,
And a following flock behind Him.

O love of the sheep, O life from the dead,
O strength of the faint and the fearing!
A Shepherd is King, and His Kingdom will come,
And the day of His coming is nearing!

VIII

ARE THERE SIGNS, AND CAN WE SAFELY INTERPRET THEM?

A CHRISTIAN woman in the Middle West wrote to a friend in the summer of 1936: "Flood—forest fires—famine! I am so glad I'm only passing through, pilgrim and alien. I wish I understood exactly what our Father is saying by all this unprecedented disaster."

And think of what has happened *since* then! Disasters in the natural world around the globe; "acts of God" and acts of Satan; crimes and atrocities by the hands of men, youth, even children, that make the blood run cold and hearts fail; wars of unparalleled ferocity; the throne of the greatest empire on earth abdicated for the love of a twice-divorced woman; labor troubles and strikes forced through in contemptuous defiance of the law; atheism and blasphemy rampant—does it all mean anything? Are these world-convulsing phenomena meaningless, or are they signs?

Statesmen and journalists, some of whom are not Christians and who pay little if any attention to Bible prophecy, "are in their generation wiser than the children of light" (Luke 16:8), for they see things more clearly than do some Christians. Walter Lippman, that brilliant Jewish journalist and essayist, wrote two years ago in his column, "Today and Tomorrow" (New York *Herald-Tribune*, March 2, 1935): "The signs are multiplying that the stage is set for an event of world-wide importance and of unpredictable consequences." Nineteen centuries ago the Lord described this "setting of the stage" for the end of the age and event of world-wide importance—but the consequences were not "unpredictable" to the Lord. He told us plainly that these things would happen, and what the result would be.

Within recent years Lord Robert Cecil of Great Britain said: "I read the papers with increasing uneasiness. I believe we are headed straight for one of the greatest disasters that has ever come upon mankind." And that canny Welshman, Lloyd George, former Prime Minister of Britain, did not hesitate to express his fear: "I cannot say what is going to happen to the world. I am alarmed. I will go so far as to say I am frightened at what will happen."

In 1929 a chapter of the American Red Cross published a leaflet entitled, "The Rising Curve of Disasters in the United States." Facts and statistics were given showing the steadily increasing number and severity of so-called natural disasters in five-year periods from 1905 to 1929. Disasters of this sort are called by insurance companies and in legal contracts "acts of God," as indeed they are. In the five five-year periods the disasters ran as follows: 16, 23, 67, 271, 397. A similar statistical report since 1929 would, of course, far exceed the startling character of the events before then.

People who do not look to God or to His "more sure word of prophecy" (2 Pet. 1:19) are seeing signs and interpreting them. The Philadelphia *Inquirer* of December 27, 1936, gave a full page of "Astonishing Predictions for the Year 1937," and deported the sign-seeing of astrologers and pyramidologists, declaring that there was "remarkable concurrence of different schools of prophecy in forecasting for the new year," and that momentous events had already begun to occur.

There are plenty of false prophets, and some of these stumble on the truth while others speak nothing but lies. God told one of His own true prophets to "prophesy against the prophets of Israel that prophesy . . . out their own hearts." This was the word: "Thus saith the Lord God; Woe unto the foolish prophets, that follow their own spirit, and have seen nothing!" (Ezek. 13:1-3.) Yet God's own people, like some of His people today and like the blind, unsaved world, gladly followed false prophets and rejected God's own infallible prophecies. There is a tragic story of this in Jeremiah 42.

But when we face today the question of "signs of the times" and their interpretation, we must face in all seriousness the question asked by sincere and honest people, both Christians and non-Christians: *Are there really signs show-*

ing that the Lord's return is near? And if indeed there are such signs, *Have we any right to believe that we can interpret them with safety or accuracy?* Many Christian people in earlier times, it is pointed out, were entirely mistaken in thinking that the end of the age had come and that the Lord's return was soon to occur. Why may not we be mistaken also, if we connect the strange and startling things that are happening before our eyes with the Second Coming of Christ?

These are fair questions. They must not be ignored, or pushed aside as only expressions of skepticism.

There is a sure, infallible answer in God's Word. And let us remember, as was shown in the first chapter, that prophecy is not only contained in the Word of God, but that the Bible is chiefly a book of prophecy. Predictive prophecy is its great, dominant note, from Genesis to Revelation. Let us look to it with confidence, therefore, to answer these questions that so many are asking today.

Are there really any "signs of the times," and if there are, is it safe or right for us to attempt to interpret them?

Unbelieving Pharisees and Sadducees once came to the Lord Jesus, in crafty hypocrisy, "and tempting desired him that he would shew them a sign from heaven." His answer is most significant:

He answered and said unto them, When it is evening, ye say, It will be fair weather: for the sky is red. And in the morning, It will be foul weather to day: for the sky is red and lowring. O ye hypocrites, ye can discern the face of the sky; but can ye not discern the signs of the times? (Matt. 16:1-3).

So the Lord recognized and declared that there are signs; and not only that, but He sternly rebuked God's people for their failure to interpret "the signs of the times."

Our question is answered, with authority and finality. The Lord continued: "A wicked and adulterous generation seeketh after a sign; and there shall no sign be given unto it, but the sign of the prophet Jonas." We know from other Scriptures what he meant. "For as Jonas was a sign unto the Ninevites, so shall also the Son of man be to this generation" (Luke 11:30). "For as Jonas was three days and three nights in the whale's belly; so shall the Son of man be three days and three nights in the heart of the earth" (Matt. 12:40). The resurrection of Christ from the dead was the great "sign" for His generation and for all generations. Some fail to interpret it; some interpret it correctly, and God's blessing rests upon them for seeing the sign and understanding it.

Again, the Lord's disciples "came unto him privately" and asked Him: "what shall be the sign of thy coming, and of the end of the world [consummation of the age]?" (Matt. 24:3.) The Lord answered their question plainly, and told them in great detail what the signs were to be,— but He began by the warning, "Take heed that no man deceive you." There were to be plenty of false signs, one of which was to be the appearance of false Christs; this is taking place before our eyes today and is fulfilling the prophecy that it "shall deceive many."[1]

In that great prophetic Olivet discourse (Matt. 24, 25; Mark 13; Luke 21) the Lord predicted the characteristic events of the course of the entire age or dispensation that had begun with His first advent and will be ended by His second advent, and He also foretold the signs that would declare the very ending of the age and herald His personal return in glory. That last great event must be preceded by the rapture, or catching away of the Church to meet the Lord in the air (1 Thess. 4:16, 17; 1 Cor. 15:51-54). Therefore, if the signs of the Lord's return in glory have begun to appear, His return for His Church is still nearer, and may be at any moment. But the Lord warned us against being misled by the arising of "false Christs, and false prophets," who "shall shew great signs and wonders; insomuch that, if it were possible, they shall deceive the very elect" (Matt. 24:24). There is no excuse for our being deceived, for the Lord says immediately, "Behold, I have told you before."

And the culmination and climax of signs is this:

And then shall appear the sign of the Son of man in heaven: and then shall all the tribes of the earth mourn, and they shall see the Son of man coming in the clouds of heaven with power and great glory (Matt. 24:30).

[1] See Chapter XIX.

Later chapters take up in detail many of the signs of the times in which we live, plainly and unmistakably predicted in the prophetic Scriptures and now taking place with equal plainness and beyond all question before our eyes. But this should be said before going on later with an examination of these convincing signs. The difference between this present day and earlier generations, when some of God's people have mistakenly supposed that, because of certain signs, the end of the age was upon them and the Lord's return was at hand, is simply this: in our generation, for the first time since the risen Lord ascended to Heaven, *all the predicted major signs of the end of the age are synchronizing.* One or more of these signs have occurred in earlier generations; *never before have they all occurred simultaneously,* as we see them today. This is of profound significance, and undoubtedly is the reason why the prophetic Scriptures are being studied and are unsealed, opened, to vast numbers of God's people throughout the world as never before, in fulfillment of the prophecy to Daniel: "But thou, O Daniel, shut up the words, and seal the book, even to the time of the end: many shall run to and fro, and knowledge shall be increased" (Dan. 12:4). This divine word was given to Daniel at the end of his detailed predictions, or "history written in advance," down to the time of the Lord's return.

As for the synchronizing of the divinely predicted and infallible signs of the end of the age, here is a remarkable fact, brought out some years ago by D. M. Panton of England, Editor of *The Dawn.* The Lord said that wars would continue during the entire age of grace, as they have. But then He gave a sign of the end: "Nation shall rise against nation, and kingdom against kingdom: and great earthquakes shall be in divers places, and famines, and pestilences" (Luke 21:10, 11). Within the single decade from 1912 to 1922 Four Sore Judgments from God have come upon this earth: the greatest war in the history of the world; the greatest earthquake in the history of the world; the greatest famine in the history of the world; the greatest pestilence in the history of the world. Is not this an impressive and significant synchronizing of signs of the times, and can it have but one meaning? Details of these four judgments are taken up in Chapter XII, "Four Unprecedented Signs."

The year after the World War ended, Dr. Lewis Sperry Chafer, the well known Bible teacher and student of Bible prophecy, made an address in Atlanta, Georgia, before the Laymen's Missionary Movement Convention, on "Seven Biblical Signs of the Times." [2] The seven great signs of the end of the age predicted in the Scriptures, and discussed by Dr. Chafer, are these:

1. The Jewish Sign.
2. The Gentile Government Sign.
3. The Jerusalem Sign.
4. The Unveiled Prophecy Sign.
5. The Material Earth Sign.
6. The Apostasy Sign.
7. The Commercial Sign.

The Scriptural examination of these signs, and the facts relating to them in current events, make a rewarding and convincing study.

Signs have a very large place in the Scriptures, as any concordance will show. And signs were divinely given to illuminate, reveal, disclose, not to mystify or conceal. They were given to be studied, understood, and interpreted. The last book of the Bible, The Revelation, is predictive prophecy set forth by many signs, and it has puzzled or baffled many; yet, as has often been pointed out, the very title of the book shows that it is not a book of concealment but of revealing. The first verse tells us that it is "The Revelation of Jesus Christ, which God gave unto him, to shew unto his servants things which must shortly come to pass; and he sent and signified it by his angel unto his servant John." That word "signified" could be read "sign-ified," for the Greek verb translated "signified" is the word from which the Greek noun translated "sign" comes. The verb "signified" in Revelation 1:1 means literally "to give a sign, to indicate." Therefore we know that the Lord Jesus Christ has given us the signs of the end of the age, divinely and

[2] *Seven Biblical Signs of the Times,* by Dr. Chafer, is published as a booklet by the Bible Institute Colportage Association, 843 N. Wells Street, Chicago, 20 cents.

infallibly, so that we may understand and interpret them when they come to pass.

God wants us to be both solemnized and cheered by the signs of the times. They show His necessary and righteous judgment upon sin and a Christ-rejecting world. But they show also His glorious and undefeatable plan and purpose to redeem the world that He created, and to send His Son to rule over it in person. So the Lord Himself tells us, after describing the signs that we are now beginning to see, and after predicting "distress of nations, with perplexity . . . men's hearts failing them for fear, and for looking after those things which are coming on the earth," nevertheless, "when these things begin to come to pass, then look up, and lift up your heads; for your redemption draweth nigh" (Luke 21:25-28).

IX

GOD'S GREATEST SIGN — THE JEW

WITHOUT the firing of a shot by the British, Jerusalem was surrendered to General Allenby on December 11, 1917, and the control of the Holy Land for centuries by the Turks passed to a Christian nation. Students of Bible prophecy were thrilled and awed. I remember a letter that I had from my beloved friend and teacher, Dr. C. I. Scofield, in which he said: "Now for the first time we have a real prophetic sign."

God's greatest miracle, as was brought out in an earlier chapter, is the resurrection of the dead—"Christ the first fruits; afterward they that are Christ's at his coming" (1 Cor. 15:23), and finally the resurrection of all the dead before the "great white throne" (Rev. 20:11, 12). But— apart from this greatest of miracles, the resurrection—God's greatest sign through the ages has been, and will continue to be, the Jew.

This is not a mere human opinion. God settles it by a question he asked of Israel more than three thousand years ago:

For ask now of the days that are past, which were before thee, since the day that God created man upon the earth, and ask from the one side of heaven unto the other, whether there hath been any such thing as this great thing is, or hath been heard like it? Did ever people hear the voice of God speaking out of the midst of the fire, as thou hast heard, and live? Or hath God assayed to go and take him a nation from the midst of another nation, by temptations, by signs, and by wonders, and by war, and by a mighty hand, and by a stretched out arm, and by great terrors, according to all that the Lord your God did for you in Egypt before your eyes? Unto thee it was shewed, that thou mightest know that the Lord he is God; there is none else beside him (Deut. 4:32-35).

God has done for the Jews, and will yet do for them, what He never has done and never will do for any other nation or race of mankind. Here are seven great privileges God has arbitrarily given to Israel and to no other people: "the adoption, and the glory, and the covenants, and the giving of the law, and the service of God, and the promises; whose are the fathers, and of whom as concerning the flesh Christ came, who is over all, God blessed for ever" (Rom. 9:4, 5).[1]

Is any further word needed to show Israel's unique glory? Then this:

The Lord hath avouched thee this day to be his peculiar people, as he hath promised thee, and that thou shouldest keep all his commandments; and to make thee high above all nations which he hath made, in praise, and in name, and in honour; and that thou mayest be an holy people unto the Lord thy God, as he hath spoken (Deut. 26:18, 19).

As Israel's land, divinely covenanted to her by the Lord as her possession forever, is in God's sight and plans the geographical center of the world and "the glory of all lands" (Ezek. 20:6), so Israel as a people is God's center and determinant for all peoples, as shown in this astounding declaration:

When the Most High divided to the nations their inheritance, when he separated the sons of Adam, he set the bounds of the people according to the number of the children of Israel (Deut. 32:8).

Such Scriptures as these lift out of the realm of doubt or human opinion the preëminence of the Jew. God has called His people; God has given them great and unique gifts; and "the gifts and calling of God are without repentance" (Rom. 11:29).

How shocking, therefore, to find in Sunday school lesson helps, for the study of Christian teachers and classes, statements denying these infallibly revealed facts. There are many lesson helps which, with *The Sunday School Times*, accept unquestioningly what the Word of God says. But

[1] The statement, "whose are the fathers," is a fact of their ancestry, and different from the seven divine honors listed in this passage.

when the call of Abram was studied in April, 1932, a lesson article in a denominational paper made these statements:

Into the life of those times . . . this old legend is so woven that it earns a place for itself as a part of the actual story of human origins . . . a hero tale fragrant with the aroma of ancestor worship. . . . The evolution of religion . . . is marked by the emergence of pioneer souls who strike out upon their own lonesome quest for a clearer view of God . . . Abram, Ikhnaton, Moses, Amos, Zarathustra, Gautama, Jesus, Mohammed, Augustine, Wesley, Roger Williams—the list is a long one of pioneers, dissenters, radicals, founders of sects.

May God safeguard our Sunday schools from the teaching of such deadly denials of His Word!

Christ is the theme of the Bible. Prophecy, centering about Christ, is the dominant note of the Bible. The Second Coming of Christ—being His personal, visible, bodily return to establish His Kingdom on earth and to reign over Israel and the world for a thousand years, after which will come "a new heaven and a new earth" (Rev. 21:1)—is the goal, climax, and consummation of Bible prophecy. As we study God's greatest sign, the Jew, let us remember that Israel never can fulfill God's destiny for her until Christ comes again. His Coming is near; the Scriptures make this plain, as was shown in the last chapter, and as will be brought out in later chapters; and the Jews as a people, while many of them do not realize it, are furnishing profoundly impressive evidence of this. The fig tree is one of the Bible symbols for the Jew, and the Lord said in His great prophetic discourse on Olivet: "Now learn a parable of the fig tree; When his branch is yet tender, and putteth forth leaves, ye know that summer is nigh" (Matt. 24:32). Israel is indeed putting forth leaves, as the next chapter shows. Let us look at a few of the many prophetic Scriptures, revealing God's plans and purposes, blessings and judgments, for His great "sign," the Jew.

The Jews are a Semitic, or Shemitic, people. That word takes us back to Shem, the son of Noah who was blessed of God beyond the other two sons. Ham (or Canaan) was to be "a servant of servants"; Japheth was to "dwell in the tents of Shem"; but "Blessed be the Lord God of Shem; and Canaan shall be his servant. God shall enlarge Japheth, and he shall dwell in the tents of Shem; and Canaan shall be his servant" (Gen. 9:25-27). From Shem descended the Jews. There is our first prophecy of "the Jew first" (Rom. 1:16).

Four centuries later came the call and founding of the Jewish race through Abraham. A new dispensation had begun, that of Promise, as God called Abram out of his land and away from his kindred and spoke this great prophecy:

And I will make of thee a great nation, and I will bless thee, and make thy name great; and thou shalt be a blessing: and I will bless them that bless thee, and curse him that curseth thee: and in thee shall all families of the earth be blessed (Gen. 12: 2, 3).

Then came the promise and prophecy of the land: "Unto thy seed will I give this land" (Gen. 12:7).

This basic prophecy-promise was reiterated and enlarged by God to Abraham, Isaac, and Jacob (Israel), as when "the Lord make a covenant with Abram, saying, Unto thy seed have I given this land, from the river of Egypt unto the great river, the river Euphrates" (Gen. 15:18).

There were detailed prophecies of both the natural and the spiritual descendants of Abraham: "And I will make thy seed as the dust of the earth: so that if a man can number the dust of the earth, then shall thy seed also be numbered" (Gen. 13:16). "Look now toward heaven, and tell the stars, if thou be able to number them: and he said unto him, So shall thy seed be" (Gen. 15:5).

These prophecies have had partial fulfillment through the centuries, but not yet the complete fulfillment that awaits the Lord's return. Under David and Solomon, Israel possessed a great deal of the covenanted land; Abraham's natural posterity has become multiplied millions. Through Israel's Messiah, "Jesus Christ, the son of David, the son of Abraham" (Matt. 1:1), many nations of the earth have been blessed and there are unnumbered millions of Abraham's spiritual posterity.

Abram was told that "thy seed shall be a stranger in a land that is not theirs, and shall serve them; and they shall afflict them four hundred years; and also that nation, whom they shall serve, will I judge: and afterward shall they come out with great substance" (Gen. 15: 13, 14). Two centuries later this prophecy's fulfillment began, and then, in God's time, came the miraculous exodus (Exod. 14).

Such blessings as no other nation has ever known were prophesied by God for Israel; and also such judgments or divine curses as no other nation has ever known,—the latter because of Israel's deliberate, persistent, and continued apostasy in spite of her exalted favor in God's sight and purpose. The long chapter in Deuteronomy 28 sets down these predicted blessings and cursings. Many of the blessings came to Israel under David and Solomon—but not all, for they yet await the return of Israel's Messiah, and Israel's turning to Him. Many of the tragic, desolating judgments have fallen upon Israel, and are striking again in the white heat of revived and increasing anti-Semitism.

Has ever another people, for example, known any such judgment and desolation as this?

And the Lord shall scatter thee among all people, from the one end of the earth even unto the other; and there thou shalt serve other gods, which neither thou nor thy fathers have known, even wood and stone. And among these nations shalt thou find no ease, neither shall the sole of thy foot have rest: but the Lord shall give thee there a trembling heart, and failing of eyes, and sorrow of mind: and thy life shall hang in doubt before thee; and thou shalt fear day and night, and shalt have none assurance of thy life: in the morning thou shalt say, Would God it were even! and at even thou shalt say, Would God it were morning! for the fear of thine heart wherewith thou shalt fear, and for the sight of thine eyes which thou shalt see (Deut. 28: 64-67).

This prophecy has been fulfilled with poignant fidelity in Spain and Russia in earlier times, and in Germany today.

On July 27, 1936, there was no wailing of the Jews at the Western Wall of Solomon's Temple—the eve of the ninth of Ab. *The Advent Witness* of London called attention to this and quoted from a Palestine paper, *Haboker:*

To-night, the eve of the Ninth of Ab, will be the first in the long history of our people that we shall not mourn at the ruin of the Western Wall. Many hundreds of years have witnessed the weeping of the mourners of Zion at this shrine. In the darkest days, even in the time of Adrianus, when Jews were forbidden to enter Jerusalem, this right was vouchsafed them, the single privilege of mourning at the Wall once a year, on the eve of the Ninth of Ab.

This tradition has never been interrupted for more than a thousand years before now. This year, under the administration of the great British nation, the Jewish people is unable to visit the Western Wall. Had our neighbors [the Arabs] been denied a single opportunity of worship, the opportunity of visiting a single mosque, what cables of protest would have buzzed round the world! What a furor would have been aroused at such persecution and oppression and offense to conscience! What shall we do? Shall we also protest that in our own "National Home" we are denied the century-old privilege of reading the testament of the destruction at the Wall? . . . We know the force of precedent in this land. If but once this right is withheld us, and that on the eve of the Ninth of Ab, the denial may become more permanent.

The Wall, dark and unattended to-night, is a sign of the time (even the Jews can see something significant in this imposed silence, although such silence was imposed in the interest of peace). We shall have to dwell on this "small" matter, too, when we come to chronicle the history of the "Yishuv" (Jews in Palestine) in the year 5696.

The Advent Witness comments: "The Wailing Wall is mentioned in Scripture. 'Their heart cried unto the Lord, O wall of the daughter of Zion, let tears run down like a river day and night: give thyself no rest; let not the apple of thine eye cease" (Lam. 2:18). Why has God for the first time allowed man to impose silence on His ancient people and thus interfere with the inspired word of His servant Jeremiah, "Let tears run down like a river day and night"? Are we not justified in believing that something remarkable will happen soon concerning the Jew, the Temple area site, and that ancient Wailing (Western) Wall?"

But the greatest heartbreak comes in the realization that God's highly favored and uniquely chosen people Israel *have not yet had their worst sufferings.* For their worst and greatest apostasy, as predicted in the Scriptures, is still ahead. When their Messiah came to them, they rejected and crucified Him. He said to them plainly: "I am come in my Father's name, and ye receive me not: if another shall come in his own name, him ye will receive" (John 5:43). That "other" is yet to come, the Beast or World-Emperor, who will be received and worshiped by the Jews as their Messiah, and also as divine by most of mankind. This will call down the awful judgments of the Great Tribulation, involving the whole earth but distinctively "the time of Jacob's trouble" (Jer. 30:7; see Scofield Reference Bible, note on Rev. 7:14).

Turning back again to Israel's Old Testament experience, we find her apostasy predicted by Moses even before she entered the land (Deut. 31:16-20); and then, many centuries later, came predictive warnings from the prophets, including the detailed prophecy of her seventy-year captivity in Babylon (Jer. 25:11).

The return from the Babylonian captivity after the seventy years is predicted with equal definiteness (Jer. 25:12), and the fulfillment of this prophesied return is recorded (2 Chron. 36:23; Ezra 1:1; Dan. 9).

There is a midnight darkness in these prophetic pictures of Israel, and there is a noonday brightness. But the bright and glorious prophecies more than offset the dark and tragic ones. "Hath God cast away his people? God forbid" (Rom. 11:1). One of the greatest prophecies in all the Bible—and it was uttered by inspiration more than two and a half millenniums before the event, which has not yet come to pass, is this:

Therefore, behold, the days come, saith the Lord, that they shall no more say, The Lord liveth, which brought up the children of Israel out of the land of Egypt; but, The Lord liveth, which brought up and which led the seed of the house of Israel out of the north country, and from all countries whither I had driven them; and they shall dwell in their own land (Jer. 23: 7, 8).

We are beginning to see Israel's return to the Land in unbelief, as the notable volume by George T. B. Davis shows with convincing power.[2] The next chapter discusses Zionism and its relation to Bible prophecy.

---

[2] *Rebuilding Palestine According to Prophecy,* with many full-page illustrations from recent photographs in Palestine. (The Million Testaments Campaigns, 1505 Race Street, Philadelphia, 25 cents paper, 50 cents cloth.)

For even the great tribulation, "the time of Jacob's trouble," will not destroy God's people Israel. In the very verse that tells us of the coming of this great tragedy, when Jeremiah exclaims: "Alas! for that day is great, so that none is like it," the prophet continues:

But he [Jacob] shall be saved out of it. For it shall come to pass in that day, saith the Lord of hosts, that I will break his yoke from off thy neck, and will burst thy bonds, and strangers shall no more serve themselves of him: but they shall serve the Lord their God, and David their king, whom I will raise up unto them. Therefore fear thou not, O my servant Jacob, saith the Lord; neither be dismayed, O Israel: for, lo, I will save thee from afar, and thy seed from the land of their captivity; and Jacob shall return, and shall be in rest, and be quiet, and none shall make him afraid. For I am with thee, saith the Lord, to save thee: though I make a full end of all nations whither I have scattered thee, yet will I not make a full end of thee (Jer. 30:8-11).

Let us thank God for this prophecy, and for Paul's sure word:

And so all Israel shall be saved: as it is written, There shall come out of Sion the Deliverer, and shall turn away ungodliness from Jacob: for this is my covenant unto them, when I shall take away their sins (Rom. 11:26, 27).

Do you know any Jews today? Do you love them? If they do not yet know their Messiah and Saviour, are you praying for them, asking God to save them for Christ's sake that they may be, like Paul, "born out of due time"? (1 Cor. 15:8.) For, let us never forget, the Jew is the apple of God's eye. "For thus saith the Lord of hosts . . . he that toucheth you toucheth the apple of his eye" (Zech. 2:8). And the time is coming when any Gentile, any man anywhere, who knows a Jew will be proud of it! The Jew will be the most admired, the most sought after, the most beloved and lovable, of all the men of earth.

Thus saith the Lord of hosts; In those days it shall come to pass, that ten men shall take hold out of all languages of the nations, even shall take hold of the skirt of him that is a Jew, saying, We will go with you: for we have heard that God is with you (Zech. 8:23).

X

IS THE FIG TREE BUDDING?

IT WAS an open air Bible class on a Sunday morning at Mount Hermon, in the Santa Cruz mountains, California, in the summer of 1934. Dr. Francis W. Russell was leading us in a rich study of "Christ in the Scriptures." As we sat there, our attention held by the theme and its unfolding, I heard the roar of an airplane motor overhead. A moment later there came through the still air the long-drawn-out whistle of a distant train. It flashed into my mind that here was a parable: the airplane, high in the heavens, was the Church of Christ whose dwelling place is in the heavenlies in Christ (Eph. 1:3); while the train, holding to its earthly course in its appointed way on the steel rails, was Israel, God's chosen people appointed to earthly blessings granted to no other race. And our Bible lesson was telling us of the Christ of all the Scriptures, Head and Lord of the Church, Messiah and King of Israel.

The return of this Lord and King is the great hope both of the Church and of Israel. The divinely ordained destiny of each awaits Christ's Coming. The glorious goal of neither one can be attained until Christ comes again. But this is a sure, unfailing hope, and the signs of its near fulfillment are multiplying before our eyes.

The fig tree is a Scriptural symbol or type of the Jew.[1] In His great Olivet discourse, answering His disciples' question as to "what shall be the sign of thy coming, and of the end of the world [consummation of the age]?" (Matt. 24:3), the Lord said: "Now learn a parable of the fig tree; when his branch is yet tender, and putteth forth leaves, ye know that summer is nigh." Is the fig tree beginning to put forth leaves? Is there any reason to believe that the fig tree is now budding?

[1] See *Does "Fig Tree" Mean the Jews?* p. 169.

Yes, there are impressive evidences of this—indeed, overwhelmingly convincing signs. There has been a putting forth of leaves in our generation that has not occurred before in the nineteen centuries since our Lord spoke those words.

In 1882 a Jewish physician living in Russia, Dr. Leo Pinsker, published in Berlin a stirring "Appeal" to the Jews to stop their wanderings and find a national home of their own. But he was blind to Israel's own Scriptures, for he said:

We must, above all, not dream of restoring ancient Judea. We must not attach ourselves to the place where our political life was once violently interrupted and destroyed. The goal of our present endeavors must not be the "Holy Land" but a land of our own. . . . Thither we shall take with us the most sacred possessions which we have saved from the shipwreck of our former fatherland, the God-idea and the Bible.

Just at that time, however, the first of the Edmond de Rothschild settlements in Palestine was established near Joppa, called Rishon-le-Zion, or "First in Zion."

The birth pangs of Zionism had begun, and a dozen years later an Austrian Jewish lawyer, Theodore Herzl, published his momentous article on "The Jews' State." As a result, in 1897 the first Zionist Congress was held at Basel, Switzerland, under Herzl's leadership. The platform adopted began: "Zionism aims at establishing for the Jewish people a publicly and legally assured home in Palestine." [2]

Things moved slowly, but the movement did not die out. Herzl died in 1904, but other leaders went on with the work, and in 1909 the Jewish city Tel Aviv, near Jaffa (Joppa), was founded. Five years after the founding of Tel Aviv the World War began, and before it ended Palestine was freed by a Christian nation from the domination of the Turks, and the way was open for Zionism's dreams to be realized. Today Tel Aviv is a flourishing all-Jewish city of

[2] The writer is indebted for some of the facts in this chapter to two valuable books: *God Speaks Again in Palestine,* by P. N. Sigler (Modmir Publishing Co., 1020 Reibold Bldg., Dayton, Ohio, $1.25); and, *Rebuilding Palestine According to Prophecy,* by George T. B. Davis; (The Million Testaments Campaigns, 1505 Race Street, Philadelphia, 25 cents paper, 50 cents cloth postpaid).

125,000 people, having the largest population of any city in Palestine, not even excepting Jerusalem. One of its modern, electric lighted streets along which busses and automobiles speed and which is lined with beautiful buildings is Allenby Road, named for the great British Field Marshal who took Jerusalum without the firing of shot.

The development and prosperity of Palestine in recent years have been amazing—plainly under the supernatural touch of God's hand. A large area recently acquired by the Jews for development is in the Lake Huleh (Waters of Merom) region, about 14,000 acres, which when reclaimed will provide for some 30,000 people. The London *Christian* says that, when the Jewish Agency approached a British bank in Jerusalem for a loan of half a million pounds to buy this land and for other purposes, there was considerable opposition among members of the bank board. Some felt that there was insufficient security, and that there might be offense to other clients if such a loan were made to the Jews. After listening to various arguments the chairman sent for a Bible. To the astonishment of all he read aloud from Ezekiel 36:8-11:

But ye, O mountains of Israel, ye shall shoot forth your branches, and yield your fruit to my people of Israel; for they are at hand to come. For, behold, I am for you, and I will turn unto you, and ye shall be tilled and sown: and I will multiply men upon you, all the house of Israel, even all of it: and the cities shall be inhabited, and the wastes shall be builded: . . . and I will settle you after your old estates, and will do better unto you than at your beginnings: and ye shall know that I am the Lord.

The chairman continued: "Now the Lord is for this people; who is against them?" The loan was approved unanimously.

Such is the public confidence in the future of Palestine that when, early in 1936, the Rutenberg Electric Company offered 600,000 new shares at one pound each, the demand was such that the offer had to be closed a few hours after it was opened, applications having been received for £18,-000,000 worth of stock, the issue being thus over-subscribed thirty-one times.

A dramatic incident, now well known, played a central part in opening the land of Abraham again to his descendants. The British leaders, soon after the beginning of the World War, had become alarmed over their inadequate supply of high explosives; acetone was demanded in enormous quantities, and could not be had. A loyal British Jew, Dr. Chaim Weizmann, Professor of Chemistry in the University of Manchester, discovered a way of producing acetone in large quantities, and he reported this to the British officials just when conditions seemed hopeless. He was asked by the Prime Minister, Lloyd George, to name his price for his discovery. Now it so "happened" that Weizmann was the head of the Zionist Movement at that time, and he answered that he asked nothing for himself, but that a military expedition should be sent to Palestine to expel the Turks, and the settlement of the country by the Jews should be encouraged and facilitated. The British Government agreed, with what result the whole world knows. The fig tree was putting forth more leaves.

A thrilling event in Israel's history occurred at the time of the inaugural of the new Hebrew University on the summit of Mount Scopus, just outside Jerusalem. In a great amphitheater on the side of the hill were gathered seven thousand persons to witness the ceremonies, thousands more being unable to gain admittance. Representatives were present from more than fifty leading institutions in all parts of the world. The inaugural address was delivered by the Earl of Balfour, author of the famous "Balfour Declaration" in which Great Britain opened Palestine as the national home for the Jews. Within sight of the amphitheater was the Mount of Olives, with its graves of countless Jewish dead. The Associated Press dispatch in the papers, recounting these facts, was significant reading. Lord Balfour spoke of the difficulties confronting the University in the use of Hebrew as a living language. Recognizing its great value in literary instruction, he asked: "But does it follow that Hebrew is fitted for modern use? There is a great difference between Isaiah and microbiology. Is the language and poetical imagination of Isaiah fitted to deal with the laboratory work which is going to render this spot illustrious?" He then said that he had been assured that this difficulty had been met, and he paid a high tribute to the work done recently by Jews in the realm of science, especially Dr. Albert Einstein. Lord Allenby, the Christian General who took Jerusalem from the Moslems, was present at the inaugural.

The Bible does not limit itself to any one figure or parable in revealing truth and in predictive prophecy, which is God's infallible writing of history in advance. One of its most dramatic pictures of Israel's future is the vision of the valley of dry bones given to Ezekiel. The prophet was carried by the Lord and set down "in the midst of the valley which was full of bones . . . and, lo, they were very dry." He was asked whether these bones could live; his answer was safe and reverent: "O Lord God, thou knowest."

Here was a vivid picture of the condition of Israel through many centuries. Then—"there was a noise, and behold a shaking, and the bones came together, bone to his bone. And when I beheld, lo, the sinews and the flesh came up upon them, and the skin covered them above: but there was no breath in them." At God's word to the four winds, "the breath came into them, and they lived, and stood up upon their feet, an exceeding great army."

God interpreted the vision to His prophet. Israel was saying then, and has said countless times since then: "Our bones are dried, and our hope is lost." But God is never hopeless; and

Thus saith the Lord God; Behold, O my people, I will open your graves, and cause you to come up out of your graves, and bring you into the land of Israel. And ye shall know that I am the Lord, when I have opened your graves, O my people, and brought you up out of your graves (Ezek. 37:12-13).

Are we not seeing the beginning of the fulfillment of this prophecy today? Israel is returning to the land in unbelief, but this very fact is a fulfillment of prophecy.[8] In God's own time, in connection with the return of Israel's Messiah, both those who are in the land and others who are still dispersed will be turned to the Lord; for God continues his prophecy to Ezekiel: "and shall put my spirit in you,

[8] See *Is Prophecy Being Fulfilled in Palestine Today?* p. 170.

and ye shall live, and I shall place you in your own land: then shall ye know that I the Lord have spoken it, and performed it, saith the Lord."

Together with the coming of the flesh upon the dry bones, and the budding of the fig tree, the prophecy and sign of anti-Semitism, or Jew-hatred, is being fulfilled in tragic intensity. It is a plainly predicted and necessary judgment of Israel's righteous God.

Even before Moses died he said to his people: "I know that after my death ye will utterly corrupt yourselves, and turn aside from the way which I have commanded you; and evil will befall you in the latter days; because ye will do evil in the sight of the Lord, to provoke him to anger through the work of your hands" (Deut. 31:29). For a while Israel was faithful to God. "Israel served the Lord all the days of Joshua, and all the days of the elders that overlived Joshua, and which had known all the works of the Lord, that he had done for Israel" (Josh. 24:31). But then, after the second generation beyond Moses, the apostasy began as "the children of Israel did evil in the sight of the Lord, and served Baalim: and they forsook the Lord God of their fathers, which brought them out of the land of Egypt, and followed other gods, of the gods of the people that were round about them" (Judges 2:11, 12). Israel's apostasy reached its dreadful climax in her rejection of her plainly predicted Messiah, the Son of God and Saviour of the world, and the nation's tragic sorrows and judgments will not be ended until she fulfills the prophecy: "They shall look upon me whom they have pierced, and they shall mourn for him, as one mourneth for his only son" (Zech. 12:10).

In the meantime, and with increasing intensity today, anti-Semitism is part of God's judgment upon Israel—but woe to the nation and the individual that is a Jew-hater! Moses predicted the hatred and contempt that other nations would have for Israel, as did Jeremiah and other prophets. "And thou shalt become an astonishment, a proverb, and a byword, among all nations whither the Lord shall lead thee" (Deut. 28:37). God spoke directly to Solomon, in warning of what would follow if he and his people turned away from the Lord: "Then will I cut off Israel out of the land which I have given them . . . and Israel shall be a proverb and a byword among all people" (1 Kings 9:7). Again: "And I will deliver them to be removed into all the kingdoms of the earth for their hurt, to be a reproach and a proverb, a taunt and a curse, in all places whither I shall drive them . . . and make them an astonishment, and an hissing, and perpetual desolations" (Jer. 24:9; 25:9).

Have you ever heard a Jew called a "sheeny"? Did you realize that, whenever you hear this expression of contempt, it is a startling and literal fulfillment of the prophecy in Jeremiah 24:9? For the word translated "a taunt" is the Hebrew *sheninah,* and there is reason to believe that the vulgar slang "sheeny" is a corruption of the Hebrew word for "taunt" as applied to the Jew. Every time a joke is made against the Jew in humorous papers, or in conversation, or in our theaters, prophecy is being fulfilled as the Jew is made "a reproach and a proverb, a taunt and a curse, in all places."

But anti-Semitism is a deadly boomerang, for God has willed it so. After describing the curses which must fall upon Israel for her apostasy from God, we have this sure word of prophecy:

And the Lord thy God will bring thee into the land which thy fathers possessed, and thou shalt possess it; and he will do thee good, and multiply thee above thy fathers. And the Lord thy God will circumcise thine heart, and the heart of thy seed, to love the Lord thy God with all thine heart, and with all thy soul, that thou mayest live. *And the Lord thy God will put all these curses upon thine enemies, and on them that hate thee, which persecuted thee* (Deut. 30:5-7).

When the Israelites left Egypt they numbered some 600,000 men, besides women and children (Exod. 12:37). Today, in spite of the many attempts to destroy them by war and persecution, it is believed that they number some sixteen or seventeen millions, and they are said to be increasing more rapidly than any other people. God's promise to Abraham, as to the vast numbers of his descendants, is being kept. But anti-Semitism increases. An Associated Press dispatch in February, 1937, stated:

The greatest exodus in all their history threatens the Jewish people today. A full third of their number—5,000,000 **or more** —would have to move to new lands if the nations of Eastern Europe carry out the anti-Semitic programs they have started. Some of Poland's politicians have demanded the evacuation **of** the whole of that country's three million Jews, one-tenth of **the** entire Polish population. . . . The Nazi drive against the Jews continues in Germany. Jewish sources assert that Roumania, Lithuania, Austria, Hungary, Iraq, and Syria are bringing more and more pressure to bear, and the Jews have nowhere to go. In the nations to which they might flee, the gates of immigration are virtually closed. Palestine, Israel's ancient home, remains their great hope, but there, too, the bars are slowly locking.

A shocking instance of the bitterness of the hatred of the Jew in Germany is this statement quoted from a secular newspaper:

Julius Striecher has set out on a new anti-Semitic crusade. Answering a question from his audience of 15,000 at Karlsruhe, he said: "The only decent Jew I ever knew was so decent that he committed suicide (Judas). I would not mind if all Jews were so decent."

In May, 1937, an Associated Press dispatch startled the world with a report of a new demand by Mussolini that Italian Jews should publicly declare themselves enemies of "International Hebrewism" or renounce their Italian citizenship and residence. Mussolini's newspaper said:

Either they must publicly declare themselves enemies—we mean enemies—of international, Masonic, subversive and, above all, anti-Fascist Hebrewism and give to their manifestations a character simply and sincerely religious, or renounce their Italian citizenship and residence.

It is inconceivable that in synagogues and communities, meetings begin with expressions of fidelity to Italy, the King and Il Duce and, at the same time, demonstrate sympathies, even though theoretical, with problems and actions hostile to Italy, to the King and to Il Duce.

The newspaper specifically condemned Italian Jewry's support of Zionism and its protests against the German Nazi Race principles.

Opposition to Nazi ideas, the paper held, are "irreconcilable with the friendship that binds us to Germany and which as objectives far more vast and fundamental than the Jewish question."

Zionism, it charged, is designed to set up another State, under British control, "in definite opposition to the Mediterranean spirit of Italy." Also, it contended, no faithful Italian subject could endorse a movement "hostile" to Arabs and Moslems after Mussolini's declared Islamic policy of friendship.

Even in Great Britain, outstanding friend of the Jews, anti-Semitism has begun to appear. A United Press dispatch from London, in April, 1937, reported:

> Many persons were badly injured and six others were arrested late today when 100 British Fascists marched with torchlights into the East End Jewish district of Aldgate. Flaming torches were flung at shops and houses in and about Whitechapel, where Jewish residents barred their doors and tossed buckets of water from upper windows to extinguish the flames.

The slow locking of the bars of Palestine against the Jews, noted in the earlier newspaper dispatch quoted, refers to the intense opposition of the Arabs in Palestine to Jewish immigration, and a recent surprising concession to this by the British Government. The Colonial Secretary, William Ormsby-Gore, stated in the winter of 1936-'37 that Jewish immigration to Palestine would be limited for six months to eighteen hundred persons. The immigration has been as high as eight thousand in a single month, and this reduction was a drastic change.

But six months later an astounding action was taken— the proposed partitioning of Palestine. The magazine *Time* (July 12 and 19, 1937) reports it in characteristic descriptions:

> At a single sitting one morning last week the new British Cabinet of beak-nosed, decisive Prime Minister Neville Chamberlain resolved that the way to end seventeen years of bickering and battle between Jews and Arabs in Palestine is to carve them up into separate countries. . . . The Cabinet last week sent Minister of Colonies William Ormsby-Gore directly over to the House of Commons to announce the partition of Palestine as a general principle, ordered released within a few days the 400-

page report on Palestine of its Royal Commission chairmanned by Earl Peel.

Arabs had no way of knowing what was in the report except from Jewish news dispatches from London which said the Royal Commission would report that "the national aspirations of the Jews and Arabs in Palestine are irreconcilable," and that a solution can be found "only in the establishment of two separate States and the division of the country between Jews and Arabs."

Jewish sources published hastily drawn maps which differed considerably. All agreed, however, that the Jewish State will be in the north of Palestine, mainly along the Mediterranean; that the Arab State will be in the south, mainly inland; that His Majesty's Government will retain for themselves a corridor running inland from the port of Jaffa to such Biblical holy places as Jerusalem and Bethlehem. Some Jewish insiders opined that this British corridor will bend north at Jerusalem and extend all the way to Nazareth, others were sure it would stop at Jerusalem. Most agreed that Judea will be given to the Arabs. . . .

In Jerusalem stacks of freshly printed placards and pamphlets proclaiming martial law were on hand, ready in case of trouble to be posted up or dropped from British bombing planes. The battle cruiser *Repulse* sped from Malta to Palestine this week, her decks carrying a full flight of airplanes. . . . In case the Arabs rise, declared Palestine's leading Zionist newsorgan, "the Jews are prepared to shed their last drop of blood in a war waged for the defense of our last hopes!"

The Jewish State is to contain nearly all the best and most fruitful land in Palestine and is to have the country's only deep-sea harbor, Haifa. Nevertheless, its relatively small area was a heavy blow last week to Jews who have come to look upon *all* Palestine as "The Jewish National Home." . . .

"In the name of God and religion," the Palestine Arab Committee of the Grand Mufti Haj Amin el Husseini of Jerusalem telegraphed to doughty King Ibn Saud of Saudi Arabia and the vigorous Imam of the Yemen, "the Arab nation of Palestine begs Your Majesties to direct support of the nation in this historical and critical situation and appeals to you . . . to do your utmost to save Palestine from the evils of Imperialism and Judaization and from being torn asunder. . . ."

"Great Britain is guilty of the gravest betrayal of a most sacred trust!" cried Rabbi Stephen Samuel Wise, President of the Zionist Organization of America. "We Jews found Palestine an almost abandoned waste. Under the mandate of Britain we transformed that waste into a high civilization! [The Report] attempts to set up another spurious Arab kingdom, strikes at the very heart of Jewish hopes and is an affront to the League of Nations."

An Associated Press dispatch, July 11, 1937, from Bagdad announces:

Premier Hikmet Suliman of Iraq today offered to fight to the death any Arab who accepts the partition of Palestine proposed by Great Britain. "To cut part of the Arab countries is to cut away part of the Arabs' heart," he announced in a statement. "We will fight any man who accepts such a proposal for his own benefit. I, myself, will fight him to the death."

But God's Word stands, and "the scripture cannot be broken" (John 10:35). A mighty return of the Jews to Palestine has begun, and startingly impressive fulfillments of prophecy have taken place there before our eyes. The Hebrew language is being spoken there again after the silence of centuries. This touching incident has been published:

One of the Jewish farmers, a man over thirty years of age, had tears running down his cheeks as he registered. I asked him, "What is it?" He said, "It is so wonderful, after all these years of hard work, I can hardly believe it. To be registered as a citizen of this my own land, by a Jewish clerk in the Government office that respects my religion, in my own Hebrew language to fill out the Hebrew blank, to discuss it in Hebrew, to be sworn in on the Hebrew Bible!"

After the World War, in the early years of the British Mandate for Palestine, a visitor in that land wrote:

A young Jewish lecturer in bio-chemistry took me around the Jewish University on Mount Scopus. He had sacrificed a good post at Berlin University to dig foundations for the Jewish colonies and carry mortar, and later to lecture to about fifteen students and do research work in cotton growing. We came out to the terrace behind the University and stood where Lord Balfour stood (they worship Lord Balfour with an affection which would, I believe, go through blood for him). The sun was setting and throwing back a glow of red light on the wild hills which went tumbling to the Jordan and to the mountains climbing beyond. It was as though all was lit in a blaze of memory.

"Look," he said, "that little break in the hills right opposite!" There it was, and at the distance at which we stood it looked about three inches broad. "That was where we first came in under Moses!" His face was transfigured, and his eyes lit with that fierce flame of love which all the winds of the ages have never been able to blow out.

As David Lloyd George said in a recent magazine article, "The Red Sea has always opened its waters at the critical hour for this persecuted people."

XI

IS MODERNISM THE GREAT APOSTASY?

BIBLE prophecy is given to us by the Holy Spirit that we may know in advance what is coming upon the Church and the world, and not be taken by surprise. But have we realized the swiftness with which some of the worst prophecies are now being fulfilled?

For example, the magazine *Time* reported (Sept. 15, 1930) a meeting in Chicago of a dozen divinity school students of different Protestant denominations which came to this astounding and blasphemous conclusion: "Christ is growing increasingly unpopular in the United States, not simply the sufferer of public apathy but the subject of downright disfavor." Only one student, and he from South India, was shocked by anything the others said. He remarked: "Is it possible that any theological students do not believe in the divinity of Jesus Christ?" The report commented: "The others excused his naiveté by his brief residence in the United States."

Some years ago a young minister submitted an article to *The Sunday School Times,* and as I read the manuscript I realized that it was on a most unusual subject. The author was attempting to show that Modernism is "The Apostasy," the great apostasy which the New Testament tells us will occur shortly before the Lord's return. Not only that, but the author made the statement that Modernism is unique among all the heresies that have come into the Church during the nineteen centuries; that no other historic heresy has had the distinctive characteristic of Modernism; and that in this great heresy that is poisoning and destroying so much of the professing Christian Church of today we have an exact fulfillment of the apostasy predicted only of the end of the age.

This thesis was challenging indeed. But was it true?

Could it be proved? The author of the article was Roy L. Aldrich, pastor of the Central Presbyterian Church of Detroit. I wrote him saying that his article interested me very much indeed, but had he made such a careful study of the leading heresies of the Church for nineteen centuries as to be able to defend his claim if it were challenged?

Mr. Aldrich replied that he had not done just this, but he would do so. Some months later he wrote me again, sending the article in revised form, and I was glad to learn that his examination of the historic heresies of the Church substantiated his claim completely. Mr. Aldrich had looked up more than two hundred and fifty sects and heresies that existed in the Church from the first century to the seventeenth; in the seventeenth century appeared the beginnings of what is called Modernism today. We published his article, "Why Modernism is 'The Apostasy,'" in *The Sunday School Times* of August 30, 1930, and I am indebted to Mr. Aldrich for the facts he brought together and for his important contribution to the study of Bible prophecy.[1]

Paul writes to the Thessalonian Church concerning the coming of "the day of Christ," or the Day of the Lord:

Let no man deceive you by any means: for that day shall not come, except there come a falling away first, and that man of sin be revealed, the son of perdition; who opposeth and exalteth himself above all that is called God, or that is worshipped; so that he as God sitteth in the temple of God, shewing himself that he is God. . . . And then shall that Wicked be revealed, . . . even him, whose coming is after the working of Satan with all power and signs and lying wonders and with all deceivableness of unrighteousness in them that perish; because they received not the love of the truth, that they might be saved. And for this cause God shall send them strong delusion, that they should believe a lie (2 Thess. 2:3-11).

The Greek word translated "falling away" is *apostasia,* or apostasy (2 Thess. 2.3). Moreover the Greek uses the definite article, "the," not "a," and the passage should read, as given in the Revised Version, "THE falling away," or

[1] The pamphlet reprint of the article, "Why Modernism is 'The Apostasy,'" by Roy L. Aldrich, may be ordered from Central Presbyterian Church, Second and Grand River, Detroit, Mich.; 3 cents a copy, $2 per 100.

"THE apostasy." It is not one among several apostasies; it is THE apostasy, the only one of the sort, which shall just precede the Lord's return.

Similarly the Greek translated "a lie" (v. 11) is "THE lie," and should be so translated. There are many lies of Satan and of men recorded in the Bible, but the great, final, climatic lie is this which apostate men shall believe just before the Lord's return, when the apostasy occurs, and a man sets himself above God and calls for worship.

We know that the Antichrist, a Satan-empowered man, will be raised up of Satan and demand and receive the worship of men shortly before Christ Himself returns to reign over this earth and be worshiped of all men. But how can men be prepared for this astounding thing, the worship of a fellow man? The *peculiar doctrine of the apostasy is that man himself is divine, that man himself is God.*

Godet writes on "Revelation" in *Johnson's Cyclopedia:* "Antichrist's theological system may be summed up in the three following theses: 1. There is no personal God without or above the universe. 2. Man is himself his own god—the god of this world. 3. I am the representative of humanity; by worshiping me humanity worships itself."

And Modernism is preparing men to believe *the* lie, during *the* apostasy, by exalting man as divine. If man is divine, there is no need for regeneration or for a Saviour.

Mr. Aldrich, who brings out these facts, quotes leading Modernists of the past generation, as follows:

The late President McGiffert of Union Theological Seminary: "Divine and human are recognized as truly one. Christ, therefore, if human, must be divine, as all men are. Christ is essentially no more divine than we are or than nature is."

Dr. John H. Boyd, a Presbyterian pastor of Portland, Ore.: "Men are what they are because of a fatal disbelief in their own divinity."

Frank C. Doan, in his book, *Religion and the Modern Mind:* "Do you ask me whether God is simply the spirit of humanity? I reply that God is essentially and simply just that."

Professor W. A. McKeever of the University of Kansas, in his book, *Man and the New Democracy:* "Man is my best expression of deity, and so I bow reverently at this shrine."

Mr. Aldrich gives brief statements of certain leading heresies of earlier centuries, and shows that none of them, which gained any recognition in the Church at large, declared the divinity of man. He recognizes also, of course, that all false religious teaching comes from Satan; and that we find the real beginning of the apostasy, or Modernism, back in the garden of Eden, when Satan lied to Eve and said that, by rejecting the word of God, "Ye shall be as gods" (Gen. 3:5). Modernism is as new as that!

The foundations of the so-called Higher Criticism, the destructive criticism of the Bible, were laid in the seventeenth century. Man's denial of the truthfulness · of any part of the Word of God means, of course, that man is setting himself above God—and that is the apostasy. So the Higher Criticism, begun in the seventeenth century, has led on to the Modernism of today, culminating in the exaltation and deification of man. And when men in general come to believe that all men are divine, it will be natural and logical for them to take the final step of worshiping one man, the Antichrist, as the personification of mankind—that is, of themselves.

We are seeing a sharply defined expression of this in the crisis in the foreign mission fields of the Far East, precipitated by the demand of the Japanese Government for universal obeisance, or worship, at the Shrines. The well known missionary, Dr. George S. McCune, was deposed by the Government General of Korea from the Presidency of Union Christian College, Pyeng Yang, and from the Principalship of the Presbyterian Boys Academy, because he refused, courteously but in uncompromising Christian testimony, to do obeisance at a Shinto Shrine as demanded by the Government. A startling outbreak and riot in a Korean mission school occurred early in 1937 because of the refusal of Christian missionaries thus to worship the spirits of human ancestors, or to recognize the deity of the emperor and the imperial line.

But is Modernism, as many deceived Christian leaders are telling us, merely a restatement of Christianity in the light of present-day conditions and needs? It is not. Any such defense of Modernism is part of "the lie." The clearest thinkers among Modernists recognize the vital, eternal distinction between Modernism and Christianity. A remarkably discerning statement was made editorially by *The Christian Century* of Chicago, one of the leading liberal religious journals in America, in its issue of Jan. 3, 1924:

How deep-going is the Fundamentalist-Modernist controversy? Is it an issue worth serious attention? . . . Is not the whole controversy, after all, scarcely more than a tempest in a teapot? Or are the Fundamentalists right in claiming that the issue is a grave one, going to the roots of religious conviction and involving the basic purposes and almost the genius of Christianity itself?

A candid reply to such inquiries must be one of agreement with the Fundamentalist claim. . . . Christianity according to Fundamentalism is one religion. Christianity according to Modernism is another religion. . . . For the day of neutrality has all but passed.

There is a clash here as profound as and as grim as that between Christianity and Confucianism. Amiable words cannot hide the differences. "Blest be the tie" may be sung until doomsday, but it cannot bind these two worlds together.

The God of the Fundamentalist is one God; the God of the Modernists is another. The Christ of the Fundamentalists is one Christ; the Christ of Modernism is another. The Bible of Fundamentalism is one Bible; the Bible of Modernism is another.

These words are true with a sinister, deadly meaning of which their Modernist writer was unconscious. Would that all true Christians might discern as clearly the irreconcilable issue between Fundamentalism and Modernism, and that there might come a speedy ending of the present disastrous attempts at fellowship between light and darkness.

A generation ago the critics who were repudiating Paul's theology adopted the slogan, "Back to Christ!" But the Higher Criticism no longer holds itself under any obligation even to Christ. Professor George Jackson, a well known critic, was quoted some years ago as follows:

It is now admitted on all hands—the few dissenting voices do but emphasize the general consent—that Christ's authority cannot be invoked to invalidate the findings of modern Biblical criticism; neither do we explain His language as an accommodation to the ignorance of His contemporaries. We must maintain the limitations of the knowledge of Jesus in the interests of a true Christology and of intellectual liberty.

This is shocking confirmation of a prophecy made many years ago by that beloved and true Bible expositor, Professor Franz Delitzsch, who said to his students:

Young gentlemen, the battle is now raging round the Old Testament. Soon it will pass into the New Testament field—it is already beginning. Finally, it will pass forward to the citadel of your faith—the Person of Jesus Christ. There the last struggle will occur.

But Professor Jackson's blasphemous position is logical. When once we begin to give the lie to the written Word of God, setting ourselves above God, we must, if we are consistent, go on and give the lie to the Incarnate Word, Christ Jesus Himself. That is the end of which God forewarned, that "for this cause God shall send them strong delusion, that they should believe THE lie."

It is difficult for Christian people to realize there are professing Christians today who insist that man is the final basis of religious authority. This is the subtle heart of Modernism. A Congregational minister in New England, writing in the *Atlantic Monthly* on "The Altered Basis of Religious Authority," actually says:

The final basis of religious authority for you is yourself, your mind working on all that has come down in the religious tradition of Christianity, and selecting and making your own those things which satisfy the requirements of your intelligence, of your moral judgment, of your spiritual hunger. That is a big step to take if one has not thought about it. . . . The basis of religious authority is shifting from the Bible to the individual.

The strange thing about Modernism is that it deceives so many into thinking that it is modern. Some twenty-five hundred years ago a prophet of God was given this word of the Lord: "Prophesy against the prophets of Israel that prophesy, and say thou unto them that prophesy out of their own hearts, Hear ye the word of the Lord; thus saith the Lord God; *Woe unto the foolish prophets, that follow their own spirit, and have seen nothing!*" (Ezek. 13:2, 3). The attempt to "follow their own spirit" in discerning spiritual truth, and to speak for God "out of their own hearts," which is the creed and dogma of Modernism, is just the old expression of man's sin in rejecting God and substituting himself. It means blindness instead of vision, darkness for light, death instead of life. It is a terrible word of condemnation that God must speak to all such. "Therefore thus saith the Lord God; Because ye have spoken vanity, and seen lies, therefore, behold, I am against you, saith the Lord God."

The formation of the Bible Churchmen's Missionary Society of England, in 1922, was forced by the Modernistic position of the Church Missionary Society, which had had such an honored and blessed ministry for more than a century. This great society had finally repudiated, not only the trustworthiness of the historical records of the Bible (rejected by a vote of 210 to 130), but also the truthfulness of some of Christ's utterances. The Bible Churchmen's Missionary Society was formed by members of the older society who withdrew and united in a missionary work true to the Written Word and the Incarnate Word. The first annual report of this new society said: "When from the mission field, most experienced and devoted missionaries of all denominations, came a cry of pain and anguish, a beseeching request to the Home Boards to take steps to prevent a further proclamation of modern views in the mission field, because 'such teaching is fraught with the greatest danger to the Chinese Church, threatening in the future its very existence,' then witness to despised truth became a stern necessity."

The Bishop of Birmingham, England, the Right Rev. Ernest William Barnes, in a sermon preached in Westminster Abbey has pleaded for what he calls an open mind. He says that the story of creation as set forth in Genesis cannot be accepted as solid fact, but that "people should welcome discoveries with an open mind, and reverence the great men who made them." He continues: "Stories of the garden of Eden have become for us only folklore. Darwin's triumph has destroyed the whole theological scheme.

Man is not a being who has fallen from the ideal state of perfect innocence; he is an animal who has slowly gained spiritual understanding and, with the gain, rising far above his distant ancestors." All this, of course, gives the lie to God and exalts man. That is the heart of Modernism.

Young men studying for the ministry are deliberately trained, in many of our theological seminaries, to scoff at the idea that the whole Bible is the Word of God—and thus they are trained to scoff at God. In the Bulletin of Colgate-Rochester Divinity School (November, 1931) appears the following:

> The limited idea of God in many of the Psalms is a hindrance to their use in modern worship. . . . There are strange and uncouth depictions of the deity in certain Psalms which relegate them to the list of historical relics. . . . For example, that vigorous and imaginative poem, Psalm 60 (repeated in Psalm 108), pictures God coming up to the help of His people with all the verve and swagger of a top-sergeant. The deity of this Psalm is the "buddy" God.

Mrs. Pearl Buck resigned from her work as a Christian missionary in China after publishing statements expressing her blasphemous unbelief in the Gospel, the Bible, and Christ. While still a missionary she wrote, in *Harpers Magazine* for January, 1933, an article entitled, "Is There A Case for Foreign Missions?" She spoke of orthodox Christianity as "a narrow and superstitious form of religion, and this the intelligent Chinese is loath to see fastened upon his people." She condemned the missionaries who tell the heathen, "You must believe on the Lord Jesus and your sins will be washed away." "I agree with the Chinese," she said, "who feel their people should be protected from such superstition. . . . We no longer believe that a soul can in a moment choose its eternity." In another magazine article Mrs. Buck wrote: "The serenity of the Buddha is Christ's serenity." Concerning the Lord Himself she says: "And what if he never lived? What of that? Whether Christ has a body or not, whether he had a time to be born in history and a time to die as other men have, is of no matter now: perhaps it never was of any matter."

A devoted Christian woman, not now living, who was a

teacher in the Sunday school of a well-known church (whose pastor is one of the leaders in his prominent denomination), went to her pastor one day to talk with him about doctrinal matters. She explained to him that, inasmuch as she was very old-fashioned in her beliefs and was teaching the children in the Primary Department that the Bible was just what it claims to be, she wondered whether her pastor would really want to have her continue her work there or give it up. He assured her that he wished her to stay right on in her Sunday school work there, saying: "Most assuredly I do. I believe in teaching little children the Bible stories just as they are, *and when they are older teach them the truth.*"

She asked her pastor whether he could preach Jesus Christ as the only one and sufficient Saviour from sin. The pastor replied: "I will preach Jesus Christ. I will go no further than that." Did he believe in the deity of Christ, that God was in Christ? He answered: "I certainly do, but I believe that God is in every man and woman living."

Is the exaltation and deifying of man really entering into our churches? Back in 1922 a Christian worker in Chicago wrote to a member of the *Times* staff about a fellowship supper of Sunday school officers and teachers in the Chicago church. They had applied to a well known Sunday school association for a speaker, who was sent to them—a teacher in the University of Chicago.

At the supper this speaker, intending to encourage the Sunday school workers, said they should never be disheartened in their work but think of the possibilities in the children before them. *For among those children,* said the speaker, *there might be "another Moses, another Amos, or another Jesus."*

My friend wrote to the speaker later and asked him what he meant by "another Jesus." The speaker replied, in part: "I did say, 'another Moses, another Amos, another Jesus.' Personally I am convinced that God has by no means exhausted his resources for this world's good."

It was quite in line with such apostate teaching that Dr. Harry Emerson Fosdick, almost ten years later, preached and published his notorious sermon on "The Peril of Wor-

shiping Jesus." In that sermon Dr. Fosdick actually says
of our Lord:

> He did not fear being opposed; he feared being worshiped.
> . . . It is an amazing thing that the historic Church has so
> unanimously worshiped Jesus and has so seldom stopped to
> ask what Jesus himself would think of it. . . . He does not
> want his ego idolized; he wants his cause supported. . . . In-
> deed, he never said, "Worship me!" He said, "Follow me!"

Dr. Fosdick does not explain why Christ pronounced
blessing upon all who, not having seen Him and yet believing in Him, should follow the example of Thomas when
he cried out in worship of Christ, "My Lord and my God"
(John 20:28). Nor does Dr. Fosdick comment on the inspired word of Paul concerning Christ:

> Wherefore God also hath highly exalted him, and given him
> a name which is above every name: that at the name of Jesus
> every knee should bow, of things in heaven, and things in earth,
> and things under the earth; and that every tongue should con-
> fess that Jesus Christ is Lord, to the glory of God the Father
> (Phil. 2:9-11).

Our Lord said: "Let your light so shine before men, that
they may see your good works, and glorify your Father
which is in heaven" (Matt. 5:16). The apostate Modernist says: "Let your light so shine before men, that they
may see your good works, and glorify Man."

Thoroughgoing atheists have no illusions as to the meaning of Modernism. The American Association for the Advancement of Atheism has declared:

> Much as we dislike Modernists because of their illogical
> compromising, we must recognize that, for many, Modernism
> is but a stop-over on the road to atheism. Perhaps we should
> have a little more patience with these our weaker brothers who
> are unable to go straight from orthodoxy to atheism without
> resting at the camps of liberalism along the way. Modernism
> being no abiding place for the reasoning mind, some of them
> will yet arrive.

One of our colleges conducted a "Litany of Praise" in
its Baccalaureate Service a few years ago, written by a
student and led by the president of the college, which was

simply in praise of the self-sufficiency of man, the exaltation of man, the worship of man, with no hint of the sinner's need of a Saviour or any note of praise to God in reverent worship.

A Sunday school lesson paper published by one of our denominations contains a lesson on "The Conquering Power of Faith," with these significant statements: "The man of faith believes in himself. He knows that somewhere in the world there is a work waiting for him and he has confidence in his ability to do that work thoroughly and well."

It is interesting to read that, at the International Exposition held in Paris in 1937, the Government of Irak planned to reconstruct the Tower of Babel. And what did the Tower of Babel stand for? Simply the exaltation of man. "Go to," said the builders, "let us build us a city and a tower, whose top may reach unto heaven, and let us make us a name" (Gen. 11:4).

A newspaper headline reads, "Hitler Placed Ahead of Deity." The dispatch from Berlin says that the Rev. Dr. Reimbold Krause, a leader of the extremist wing of the "German Christians," made the public declaration: "No one who asserts that God must be obeyed before men is a true citizen of the Third Reich." And in April, 1937, another dispatch from Berlin reports that General Ludendorff has "proclaimed an open battle against Christianity," and has said: "We will rid ourselves of Christian dogma and realize the mystery of the incarnation of the German people."

A small book giving an ambitious epic poem by a well known minister of an evangelical denomination came to *The Sunday School Times* for review. I glanced through it, and its closing line caught my eye: *"The coming God, whose name is man."*

The erecting of a great image of a man, to be worshiped, is a fact of Bible history and Bible prophecy. Nebuchadnezzar was the greatest earthly king this world has yet known (Dan. 2:37, 38), and he set up an image of gold to be worshiped by all peoples (Dan. 3). Dr. Scofield comments: "The attempt of this great king of Babylon to unify the religions of his empire by self-deification will be repeated by the Beast, the last head of the Gentile world dominion (Rev. 13:11-15)." The prophecy in Revelation tells us that the final Beast, or World Emperor, sets up an image of himself, with the edict "that as many as would not worship the image of the beast should be killed."

And now we keep hearing about Mussolini statues. In 1934 the Philadelphia *Inquirer* published a photograph of a "Stone statue of an 'iron man,' " showing a remarkable monumental bust of the Premier and Dictator, standing in the center of Camp Dux, where 30,000 young Italian soldiers assemble. Another statue of Il Duce was reported by Ernest Gordon in his Survey in *The Sunday School Times* (July 13, 1935), then under construction in Rome. It is to be of bronze, two hundred and thirteen feet high, higher than the Colossus of Rhodes, and to stand above the Forum of Mussolini on Monte Mario. "The statue will show the Mussolini figure with the torso and thighs swathed in lion's skin and with an eighty-foot arm raised in Fascist salute over Rome. The site on Monte Mario is being made ready with concrete reinforcement to hold up the enormous weight of the statue, a statue which will be the largest in the world, sixty-two feet higher than that of Bartholdi's 'Liberty' in New York harbor." This image is supposed to be twice the height of the image of Nebuchadnezzar.

The Dawn has reported that "a colossal figure of Lenin, of identical height [with that of Mussolini] and chromium-plated, will shortly dominate Moscow, significantly erected on the site of the Cathedral of Christ the Saviour, which was blown up at Christmas, 1931. As this huge idol will be pitched on the summit of the Palace of the Soviets, itself eight hundred feet high, its total height will be nearly a thousand feet."

The Advent Witness (London, Jan. 1937), reports that Japan has erected a statue larger even than that which Mussolini is having made, to be called, "The Merciful Goddess."

Certainly it would seem that the world is being prepared for great, awe-inspiring images, so that when the final image of the Beast is set up, and is given supernatural, Satanic powers ("and he had power to give life unto the image of the beast, that the image of the beast should both speak, and cause that as many as would not worship the image of the beast should be killed," Rev. 13:15), the majority of mankind will be ready to worship the image and "to receive a mark in their right hand, or in their foreheads," without which "no man might buy or sell, save he that had the mark, or the name of the beast, or the number of his name."

The Dawn (June, 1937) reports: "For the first time we hear of tattooed flesh in Rome. 'On a Roman baby boy,' says the Rome Correspondent of the *Times* (April 30, 1937), 'has appeared a birthmark in the form of a perfect Lictor's Fasces.' Whether a baseless superstition, or the secret act of his parents, or a Satanic miracle, Fascism already has in thought the stamping in the flesh which will one day be the world-wide sacrament of the Antichrist."

The great apostasy, the final one, is upon us. The tragedy is that it is within the churches, deceiving professing Christians, and reaching out with deadly power into the world of the unsaved. Dr. Stanley Jones, magnetic and eloquent speaker and leader in the mission field and in homelands, has said that he believes the Church needs both Modernism and Fundamentalism (that is, the Church needs both the lie and the truth, although Dr. Jones would not agree with this putting of it); and he launched ambitious plans, while touring America with the Modernistic National Preaching Mission, for a great united Church of Christ in America that shall bring together all the denominations and branches with a united front. This is just what Bible prophecy says will come at the end, a false religious coalition, accepting The Apostasy and The Lie, and heading up in the worship of the Antichrist.

If Paul's inspired word to young Timothy was needed nineteen centuries ago, how much more is it needed today!

This know also, that in the last days perilous times shall come. FOR MEN SHALL BE LOVERS OF THEIR OWN SELVES, . . . having a form of godliness, but denying the power thereof: from such turn away. . . . I charge thee therefore before God, and the Lord Jesus Christ, who shall judge the quick and the dead at his appearing and his kingdom; preach the word; be instant in season, out of season; reprove, rebuke, exhort with all longsuffering and doctrine. For the time will come when they will not endure sound doctrine; but after their own lusts shall they heap to themselves teachers, having itching ears; and they shall turn away their ears from the truth, and shall be turned unto fables (2 Tim. 3, 4).

But man's exaltation of man is but a passing incident, though a deadly one, in the ages in which God's eternal purposes shall prevail. Isaiah saw it, and uttered the sure prophecy: "The loftiness of man shall be bowed down, and the haughtiness of men shall be made low: AND THE LORD ALONE SHALL BE EXALTED IN THAT DAY" (Isa. 2:17).

XII

FOUR UNPRECEDENTED SIGNS

THE Lord had made a startling, almost unbelievable prophecy to His disciples. When they were alone with Him they said: "Tell us, when shall these things be? and what shall be the sign of thy coming, and of the end of the world [the consummation of the age]?" (Matt. 24:3).

So the disciples asked our Lord for signs of the end of the age and of His Second Coming, and He granted their request and told them what the signs should be. He was careful to caution them—and we need this caution today—that in giving unmistakable signs of the approach of these two great events He was not setting any definite time, but only enabling us to recognize events, when they should come, which would plainly show that the end of the age and the Lord's return were near. The Lord declared the infallibility of His prophecies as He said, in that great Olivet Discourse: "Heaven and earth shall pass away, but my words shall not pass away." At once, however, He added: "But of that day and hour knoweth no man, no, not the angels of heaven, but my Father only" (Matt. 24:35, 36). We have seen, in an earlier chapter, not only that our Lord declared that there are signs of coming events which can be recognized and rightly understood, but also that He sternly rebuked God's people for their failure to interpret "the signs of the times" (Matt. 16:1-3).

Four outstanding signs, or judgments, the Lord said, would be "the beginning of sorrows," or of "birth pangs" of the new age (Matt. 24:8). These are the four: "Nation shall rise against nation, and kingdom against kingdom: and there shall be famines, and pestilences, and earthquakes, in divers places."

The *Christian* (London, Eng.) published in 1922 important articles by D. M. Panton, on "Four Sore Judgments," including the incomparable phenomenon of "The Russian Famine." The facts brought together showed from the highest civil, secular, and scientific authorities, that within the single decade from 1912 to 1922 there had occurred the greatest war in the history of the world, the greatest famine in the history of the world, the greatest pestilence in the history of the world, and the greatest earthquake in the history of the world. Here were unprecedented fulfillments of the four great signs given by our Lord as "the beginning of travail" for the Millennial Age. Note some of the outstanding facts:

In 1912 there were forty-one royal dynasties in the world: in seven years twenty-four thrones—including the three greatest land empires in the world—had collapsed and vanished. It is a remarkable fulfillment of Ezekiel 21:26, 27:

Thus saith the Lord God; Remove the diadem, and take off the crown . . . exalt him that is low [democracy], and abase him that is high [autocracy]. I will overturn, overturn, overturn . . . until he come whose right it is [to reign]; and I will give it him.

The total death roll of Europe ran into ten millions, at a cost of $250,000,000,000. The complete collapse of civilization was threatened.

The Russian famine of 1921 was unparalleled. The London *Times* called it "a spectacle that is apocalyptic in its awful suggestion of collapse." Said the Archbishop of Canterbury: "Never in the history of the world has a condition of things existed comparable to the ghastly death by famine of whole millions of men, women, and children. Dr. Nansen called it "beyond all doubt the most appalling that has ever happened in the recorded history of man." And the fact that it was a direct judgment of God is seen from this: The Volga Valley, actually the most fertile land in Europe and one of the richest agricultural districts in the world, suffered a drought in 1921 in which the rainfall was less than one-fifteenth of normal. Czarist Russia, which was responsible for the most awful pogroms of the Jews since the fall of Jerusalem, was wiped out of existence soon after. The greatest famine known before this, in China in the middle of the nineteenth century, brought the death of five thousand daily; in Russia thirty thousand died of starvation every day.

But did this divine judgment bring Russia to its knees in repentance, and turn the nation to God? Far from it. Following the revolution of government in Russia we have had the spectacle, for the first time in human history, of a great nation officially committed to atheism. The facts of the blasphemous and public attacks upon God the Father, God the Son, and God the Holy Spirit are too unspeakable to. publish here—although they have been published in Russia and in many parts of the world. An anti-God campaign in Russia was conducted aggressively; an Associated Press cable from Moscow said: "The Central Council of the Militant Godless League today proclaimed mobilization of the laboring masses in Russia for shock work against religion." Recently (March, 1937) the Associated Press has reported that there is "an alarming decline" in the forces organized to stamp out religion in Soviet Russia, and that the newspaper *Izvestia,* organ of the government, asserts that the resulting situation is "intolerable." But a report has been published that after January 1, 1937, all the diplomats in the service of Soviet Russia must be members "in good standing" of the godless movement. It reminds one of the prophecy that, when God's judgments strike, men "blasphemed the name of God, which hath power over these plagues: and they repented not to give him glory" (Rev. 16:9).

Russia is perhaps the most striking fulfillment yet of the prophecy that "the kings of the earth set themselves, and the rulers take counsel together, against the Lord, and against his anointed, saying, Let us break their bands asunder, and cast away their cords from us" (Psa. 2:2, 3). A later chapter, "The Revolt Against God," gives fuller facts of this sinister sign.

The influenza that swept around the world in the autumn and winter of 1918-1919 was a pestilence, or plague, without precedent. Major Norman White, the British Sanitary Commissioner for India, said: "It is an epidemic in many respects without parallel in the history of disease" (London

Times, April 12, 1919). In December, 1918, the medical correspondent of the *Times* said: "Six million persons have perished of influenza and pneumonia during the last twelve weeks. Business has been interferred with in every country in the world, and enormous losses in trade have been suffered. This plague is five times more deadly than the war." The total world mortality was not less than twelve millions.

"And earthquakes," predicted our Lord. There have always been wars, famines, pestilences, and earthquakes; but, just as the three great signs already described have descended upon humanity with an intensity never before known, so have earthquakes. In December, 1920, occurred an earthquake in China affecting an area of fifteen thousand square miles, wiping out whole villages and towns under falling hills, engulfing many in vast landslides, and actually moving mountains. Foreign calculations ranked this earthquake as the most destructive in the history of the world.

There have been cataclysmic quakes in the years since 1920. Two years later came the terrible earthquake centering in Yokohama and Tokyo. In 1928 a statement was published that Japan had an average of fifteen earthquakes a day in the five years since the great earthquake so destructive to Yokohama and Tokyo. A meteorological observatory issued a report showing that 27,097 quakes affecting some part of Japan had been registered on its instruments since the big earthquake. More than one-third of these earthquakes, or 9,250, were perceptible to human beings. Tokyo was affected by 4,150 shocks during the five-year period, more than half of these coming during the six months following the big 1922 disaster.

On one day in 1935 (January 4) eight different earthquakes in various parts of Europe were reported. The earthquake at Quetta, India, in 1935, was terrifying and destructive; a missionary who lived through it wrote: "The earthquake came with such suddenness that the majority of those overtaken were buried under their houses without any chance of escape." The death roll piled up until it appeared that at least twenty thousand in Quetta alone had been killed.

The *Morning Post* of London published in 1927 a leading

article entitled "The Infirm Earth," tabulating the calamities that had come upon the earth since the first of that year:

In January there were earthquakes or earth tremors in Japan, Mexico, the South of France, Portugal, and on the East Coast of England. A tornado swept the United States in February, and there were seismic disturbances in Kamschatka, Shanghai, California, Central Europe, and the Channel Islands. In March occurred the disastrous earthquake in Japan, in which some three thousand lives were lost and seven thousand people injured. In April, shocks were felt in South America, the Philippines, Johannesburg, New Zealand, and Central Europe, followed in May by an earthquake in China, in June by shocks in the Crimea, and on the East Coast of the United States, whose territory was already devastated by the floods of the Mississippi. Last week came the news of the flood in Saxony, and on Monday, there was an earthquake in Palestine.

Are we not experiencing the advance tremors of that which shall come when the seventh vial of God's wrath is poured out upon the earth, "and there was a great earthquake, such as was not since men were upon the earth . . . and the cities of the nations fell . . . And every island fled away, and the mountains were not found" (Rev. 16:1, 17-20).

Just after the disastrous earthquake in Palestine in July, 1927, many were interested to note a statement made by Professor Bailey Willis, the seismological expert of Stanford University, before the British Association for the Advancement of Science at Leeds, England. He said that the Holy Land may expect to suffer from earthquakes, that the area around Jerusalem is a region of potential earthquake danger, and that "a fault line along which earth slippage may occur passes directly under the Mount of Olives." It is impressive to set this statement of a scientist alongside the inspired Word written by Zechariah five centuries before our Lord's first earthly ministry. Fortelling the Second Coming of Christ, Zechariah writes:

And his feet shall stand in that day upon the mount of Olives, which is before Jerusalem on the east, and the mount of Olives shall cleave in the midst thereof toward the east and toward the west, and there shall be a very great valley; and half of the mountain shall remove toward the north, and half of it toward the south . . . 'and the Lord my God shall come, and all the saints with thee.

Mr. Panton says, after setting forth some of the solemn and tragic facts of God's present-day judgments:

So is the Most High thundering at the conscience of mankind. It is a mystery that the Church is not prostrate on its face before God, so acute is the crisis, and so awful and imminent the danger. If these are but preliminary travail-shudders— and they *can* be no more—what will be the birth-agonies? It accentuates the tragedy (though it but confirms the prophetic page) that a section of the Church of Christ, of unknown magnitude, while these thunders are actually in its ear, begins to tread the world's infidel way. Dr. Peake's Commentary says: "We have outgrown the view that storm, famine, pestilence, plagues, and droughts are used for the punishment of nations." . . . The very consciousness of God is dying out of the faces of men. Not so have we learned Christ. The earthquake tremors thrill and throb in the heart of him who is waiting for the King.

In 1935 I had the privilege of speaking in the First Brethren Church at Long Beach, California, of which Dr. Louis S. Bauman is pastor. As I waited in the pastor's study before the service, the Assistant Pastor, the Rev. Alan S. Pearce, told me of an incident that had occurred in that study. It was at the time of the great earthquake in Southern California in May, 1933. Long Beach suffered severely in that quake, and Dr. Bauman hurried over to the church from his home to see what damage might have been done. The walls of his study are lined with book shelves running to the ceiling. While the church building, as I recall it, was uninjured, it had been shaken so severely that the study was in chaos. Books and pamphlets had been thrown to the floor from the shelves, and were scattered everywhere; cabinet doors were flung open, files were emptied and their contents lying about. As Dr. Bauman saw all this, he noticed lying on the floor, title page up, a book by the well known student of prophecy, W. Lamb of Australia, entitled, *The World in Confusion.* And on this book, standing upright, not lying flat as one would have had every reason to expect, was a wooden cross that had been presented to Dr. Bauman by his Bible class.

Surely this was no accident or coincidence! The world is in confusion and chaos about us. Men's hearts are "failing them for fear, and for looking after those things which are coming on the earth." But no earthquake can shake or move the Cross of Christ, "towering o'er the wrecks of time." God's voice is speaking to us all:

Yet once more I shake not the earth only, but also heaven. And this word, Yet once more, signifieth the removing of those things that are shaken, as of things that are made, that those things which cannot be shaken may remain. Wherefore we receiving a kingdom which cannot be moved, let us have grace, whereby we may serve God acceptably with reverence and godly fear: For our God is a consuming fire (Heb. 12:26-29).

XIII

WAR AND PEACE

WAR and peace are playing a large part in the events of today and on the front pages of our newspapers—and they play a large part in Bible prophecy. In February, 1914, I attended my first Prophetic Conference. It was called by Dr. James M. Gray, and held at the Moody Bible Institute, Chicago. Dr. C. I. Scofield was one of the speakers, and when he said, from the platform, that all Europe was an armed camp and that a great European war might break out at any moment, the newspapers reporting the conference held this "prophecy" up to ridicule. In less than six months the greatest war in history had broken upon an amazed world.

Early that same year Dr. John Clifford, an outstanding Noncomformist leader of his generation in England, had said: "The year 1913 was a year of progress. A new era is coming nearer and nearer every year. Old factions are doomed to pass. Militarism belongs to the Dark Ages, and it is not fit for our time. It must go. It is going."

Set in contrast these two predictions of two great Christian leaders, one of whom ignored the Bible and gave man's prophecy, the other, holding close to the Word, gave God's prophecy.

Not many years before 1914 I had been quite blind to the truth of the Lord's return and the great themes of Bible prophecy, and I had attended eagerly such peace or arbitration gatherings as those held annually at Lake Mohonk, N. Y., and had accepted their sage human wisdom as authoritative. I had been "shown," by leaders of those movements, that the history of international arbitration for the past century demonstrated beyond all question that there never could be another great war! But, thanks to God's gracious leading, my eyes had been opened to prophetic truth about three years before the World War burst into flame; and when it came I realized that it was a striking, stupendous fulfillment of God's infallible prophecy. Why are men so blind? Has the magnificent Peace Palace at the Hague put an end to war? It has been noted that five of the monarchs and presidents whose pictures hang upon its walls have been assassinated since the palace was built. Men who are at war with God cannot establish any permanent peace with one another.

It is a twofold fulfillment of Bible prophecy that worldwide peace is being exploited, and believed in, more and more, while at 'the same time preparations for war go on more feverishly than ever before. On the tenth birthday of the League of Nations (June, 1929) a cornerstone was laid in Geneva of another magnificent Palace of Peace. Leaders of more than twenty nations attended the ceremony, and the President of the Assembly, Dr. Guerreo of Salvador, declared the stone "well and truly laid." The Associated Press, reporting this, added that "forecasts of a glorious future were voiced in addresses." But the addresses were silent concerning the fact that the only Palace of Peace that shall last, with a stone "well and truly laid," is the one of which God has said: "Behold, I lay in Sion a chief corner stone, elect, precious: and he that believeth on Him shall not be confounded" (1 Pet. 2:6). "For other foundation can no man lay than that is laid, which is Jesus Christ" (1 Cor. 3:11).

Within the doorway of this Geneva Peace Palace are inscribed the words "Peace and Safety." What a startling and unconscious fulfillment of prophecy!

For yourselves know perfectly that the day of the Lord so cometh as a thief in the night. For when they shall say, PEACE AND SAFETY; then sudden destruction cometh upon them, as travail upon a woman with child; and they shall not escape. But ye, brethren, are not in darkness, that that day should overtake you as a thief. Ye are all the children of light, and the children of the day: . . . therefore let us not sleep, as do others; but let us watch and be sober (1 Thess. 5:1-6).

An editorial in the San Francisco *Examiner* in August, 1936, called attention to the fact that Soviet Russia, which likes to be known as the "Workers'" Paradise, is rapidly becoming the "Militarists'" Paradise. "With empty words of peace on her lips, Russia now maintains the largest military establishment in the world." Having reduced military enlistment age from twenty-one to nineteen years, Russia will have an army of 2,300,000 by 1940. "Her far-flung propagandist organizations—'Popular Fronts,' 'Student Unions,' 'Councils for the Prevention of War and Fascism,' etc., etc.—secretly foment civil wars in other countries, following the orders of Lenin, that saintly 'pacifist' of the Red Terror of 1917-1925."

An International Peace Garden has been incorporated, with a New York city office, "to promote peace and friendship among the nations." This Peace Garden is a tract of twenty-two hundred fertile acres on the boundary line between North Dakota and Manitoba. Its promoters say naïvely that this "silent testimonial" will help to "bring a sublime human sentiment—International Peace and Good Will—within the realm of possibility." The project was launched at Toronto in 1929; its parent organization is the National Association of Gardeners. It is said to have been visited by as many as fifty thousand in a single day. And this is one of the factors to which men look to put an end to war while they ignore and deny Him who, in a garden long ago, after accepting from the Father the cup which meant His own death as the sinners' Substitute, that men might be saved, while "his sweat was as it were great drops of blood falling down to the ground," was then betrayed in that same garden by one of His own disciples and went to the cross of Calvary.

Other futile, man-made attempts to bring permanent peace, while ignoring the only way, the return of the Prince of Peace, are such organizations as the World Alliance for International Friendship through the Churches, whose leaders and members are outstanding religious liberals and Modernists; and the Peoples Mandate to Governments to End War, with headquarters in Washington, D. C., and a Committee for Western Hemisphere and Far East.

One of the most impressive assemblages of representatives of many nations in the interests of peace was that of the London Naval Arms Conference in January, 1930. The five great sea powers of civilization—Great Britain, United States, France, Italy, and Japan—met to discuss the limiting and reducing of their fleets, while fifty-seven nations had pledged themselves to the general effort in the hope of abolishing war. King George V opened the conference by an address which was broadcast by radio throughout the world. Yet even this Christian King made no mention of God on this unprecedented occasion, and no prayer was offered, although the Archbishop of Canterbury and lesser church dignitaries were present. The King, recognizing the immeasurable calamity of war and the longing of men to be done with this suicidal thing, said: "Since the Great War, all peoples have determined that human statecraft shall leave nothing undone to prevent a repetition of that grim and immense tragedy." It will take more than human statecraft to bring this miracle to pass.

Men who do not know God or the Word of God seem to think that they can avoid war by simply deciding not to have war. There are prophecies in this connection that are completely overlooked not only by the world but also by many Christians.

We often hear, for example, that the day is at hand when swords shall be beaten into plowshares. Do we remember that, before that day comes, plowshares must be beaten into swords? Here is the overlooked but unmistakably plain prophecy: "Proclaim ye this among the Gentiles; Prepare war, wake up the mighty men, let all the men of war draw near; let them come up: beat your plowshares into swords, and your pruninghooks into spears" (Joel 3:9, 10). That this prophecy looks to that which is still future is seen from the fact that it plainly relates to the very end of the age and Armageddon. Only after that final and stupendous conflict of this age has come and passed can Isaiah's prophecy be fulfilled concerning "the last days," when "the mountain of the Lord's house shall be established in the top of the mountains." Then it is that "He shall judge among the nations, and shall rebuke many people: and they shall beat their swords into plowshares, and their spears into pruninghooks: nation shall not lift up sword against nation, neither shall they learn war any more" (Isa. 2:2-4). Even in times of peace today the nations do not stop "learning war"; they have their West Point and Annapolis. But after the Lord has returned there will be neither military nor naval schools, "neither shall they LEARN war any more."

But that time has not come yet. In November, 1936, the late Arthur Brisbane had this remarkable news comment in his daily column:

The Krupp gun works in Germany celebrate their 125th birthday in a state of prosperity. After the big war, by command of the Versailles treaty, Krupp machinery for making guns was changed, nominally, to machinery for making plowshares and similar innocent utensils, and Krupps employed only ten thousand workers. Now, having gone back to gun-making, Krupps have ninety-one thousand men at work. The demand for killing machines is brisker than for plowshares in Europe just now.

Stanley Baldwin, while Prime Minister of Great Britain, made a terse statement in July, 1936. "If the world," he said, "can find no other means of settling disputes than war while bodies that fell twenty years ago are still being unearthed, then the world deserves to perish." The Toronto *Globe* made the comment: "In that single sentence is crystallized all that countless others have sought to convey by wordy, phrase-worn descriptions of the threatening European cataclysm." Mr. Baldwin spoke the truth, and it is a terrible truth. For the world, left to itself, will never find any other means of settling disputes than by the destructive tragedy of war: and we know from God's Word that the world does deserve to perish, and that it would certainly perish but for the grace of God. Christ is coming again, both to judge and to save the world.

Meanwhile the horrors of war increase and multiply. A correspondent for the Philadelphia *Inquirer* cabled in October, 1936, while watching the war in Spain:

Death dropped from the skies today among more than one hundred school children at play on the grounds of the village school house here. More than seventy of the youngsters were killed. Many of the survivors were badly injured.

I was having lunch in a cafe near the scene of the tragedy when suddenly I heard the droning of airplane motors, followed quickly by the quaking thud and resounding burst of shrapnel bombs.

My chauffeur and I rushed out of the cafe and hurried to the schoolground to help take the dead and wounded children away.

One boy's back had been blown to pieces. His horror-stricken father was carrying the body off the playfield.

A woman was carrying a little girl, the lower half of whose face had been blown away. The child was still alive. Her eyes were open and staring in fright, pain and amazement.

Frenzied mothers and father bent over the broken remains of dead and injured youngsters, searching for their children. Ambulance workers lifted the mangled dead and wounded on to stretchers.

The screams of mothers and the groans of fathers who came upon their dead or maimed children lying on the schoolground were heard above the general din and confusion.

Cool and efficient in the midst of stark tragedy that left others shaken, the members of a Scottish Red Cross ambulance unit, stationed in Parla, did their grim work quickly and quietly.

Though two of their ambulances were completely destroyed by the "silver fish"—as the big aerial bombs are called—the Scottish Red Cross workers cleared the playground of the dead and wounded within fifteen minutes.

There were really two raids on Parla. A few minutes after the first bombardment, the planes returned and dropped more "silver fish."

Another overlooked and dread prophecy is that God Himself will force war upon those who do not want war. University students in England and America are pledging themselves never to bear arms; many others are enrolled in anti-war campaigns; and the United States declares a neutrality policy,—as though these human programs could end war or even keep their sponsors out of war! The twenty-fifth chapter of Jeremiah deals first with the seventy years' captivity of Judah in Babylon, and then passes on to the end of the age, and all nat ons, and Armageddon. Hear these ominous words given by God to the prophet:

Therefore thou shalt say unto them, Thus saith the Lord of hosts, the God of Israel; Drink ye, and be drunken, and spue, and fall, and rise no more, because of the sword which I will send among you. And it shall be, if they refuse to take the cup at thine hand to drink, then shalt thou say unto them, Thus

saith the Lord of hosts; YE SHALL CERTAINLY DRINK. For, lo,
I begin to bring evil on the city which is called by my name,
and should ye be utterly unpunished? Ye shall not be unpunished: for I WILL CALL FOR A SWORD UPON ALL THE INHABITANTS
OF THE EARTH, saith the Lord of hosts (Jer. 25:27-29).

But that is not the end. God's peace cannot come until
the utter futility of man's peace has been exposed to all
mankind by the awful judgment of God's world-wide war.
Then, and then only, can be fulfilled the peace prophecies
of the New Testament and the Old, that "The Kingdoms
of this world are become the kingdoms of our Lord, and
of his Christ; and he shall reign for ever and ever" (Rev.
11:15). "For unto us a child is born, unto us a son is
given: and the government shall be upon his shoulder: and
his name shall be called Wonderful, Counsellor, The
mighty God, The everlasting Father, The Prince of Peace.
Of the increase of his government and peace there shall be
no end" (Isa. 9:6, 7).

XIV

SIGNS IN THE SKIES

IN OCTOBER, 1931, an Associated Press dispatch was headed "Gigantic New Planet Discovered Disrupting Astral Race about Sun." The dispatch was an interview with the astronomer, Dr. William H. Pickering, giving the results of years of computations and "predicting a giant unknown planet, 44,000 miles in diameter, lying far outside the present solar system limits." The planet Uranus was reported "in a perturbation," and Dr. Pickering believes its deviation "is accounted for by the existence of an unknown planet exerting a gravitational pull." "This unknown giant also seems to be affecting the actions of certain comets."

When our Lord told His disciples of the events, or signs, that should characterize the end of the age and indicate His Second Coming, He said:

> And there shall be signs in the sun, and in the moon, and in the stars; and upon the earth distress of nations, with perplexity; the sea and the waves roaring; men's hearts failing them for fear, and for looking after those things which are coming on the earth: for the powers of heaven shall be shaken (Luke 21:25, 26).

Are we now seeing some of these signs in the heavens? There are so many, of such multiplied diversity and startlingly unusual character, that the synchronizing of these with so many other signs of the end of the age given in the Scriptures cannot safely be ignored.

In January, 1936, the Los Angeles *Times* published an illustrated article entitled "Old Man Sun is Misbehaving Again." This article said:

> Watch out for sunspots! The Old Man of the Heavens is misbehaving again. He will be cutting antics for the next three

years, climaxing his strange doings in 1939. World-famous scientists have marshaled their forces to learn all they can and determine more definitely just what effects sunspots have on this world of ours. According to these scientists, we are in for a double dose of sunspots in 1939. Not only will we face the climax of what is known as the 11.1-year cycle, but also the 1400-year cycle will coincide in the same year, the first time in the history of the universe, so far as scientists are able to determine. Astronomers, volcanologists, seismologists are all active with their observations, keeping in close touch with each other and reporting every visible change on the face of the sun. . . . As was expected in many quarters, the appearance in 1935 of the vanguard of the sunspots "flow" in the inexorable march to the 1939 maximum was ushered in to the accompaniment of earthquakes in many parts of the world, notably those in Formosa, Quetta in India, Mt. Ararat in Asia Minor, with numerous others in a somewhat minor key in the United States later in the year. . . . Astronomers and volcanologists alike remember that for the first time in the history of modern sunspot observation a double maximum occurred in 1928-1929. That is, there was a period of maximum sunspots in 1928, and another, not normally due for 11.1 years, came along just one year later. Rising and falling of many islands in the Pacific, the great Long Beach earthquake, the Baffin Bay earthquake, and action by every "live" volcano in the world, were coincidents of that cycle and the period immediately afterward in which its effects were still flowing.

The Advent Witness (London, Arpil, 1937) quotes astronomers of the Ricard Observatory as having said in March of this year: "In one of the most unusual solar disturbances in thirty years a giant necklace of sun spots was draped across the face of the sun today." Some of the spots, twelve thousand miles across, are expected to produce "storms and earthquakes" on the earth before passing away.

There was a total eclipse of the sun, visible in Russia, in June, 1936; and another total eclipse, widely reported in the newspapers, in June, 1937.

A reader of *The Sunday School Times* wrote in September, 1934:

Here in Oklahoma we have been much interested in certain aspects of the sky at night for some months. I first noticed it in the late winter. Ordinarily, after dark, the sky is a dark blue, the stars are intensely bright, and objects in our yard, which is a large one, are not distinguishable; I live in a small suburban town where electric lights are not only far between and faint, but we have none in our immediate neighborhood. Along about dark I have noticed that the horizon grows light, then before you can see the change, this light or luminosity has spread all over the heavens. You cannot say that it comes from any one direction—it is just there. The sky is a fainter, lighter blue, the stars not so bright or numerous, and I can easily detect the bird bath, garden-seats, even the hammock where the shade is densest. Furthermore, shadows of the porch chairs are distinctly cast on the walls. This condition prevails all night, every night. Since it began before the drought I do not believe it is caused by dry weather or dust in the air. It is not moonlight, neither does it appear to be starlight, for their light is dimmed. My old yard man says, "Hit's jes' whah hit's mos' time for de Lord to come and hit's de glory ob Him an' de saints in glory a-shinin' th'oo de skies." I have heard no other explanation. A friend says it is discernible also near Washington. D. C.

In May, 1936, the Associated Press reported from Roseberg, Oregon:

Explosion of a meteor which flashed through the sky early today shook buildings here and awakened many residents. It afforded almost daylight brilliance, and was followed by a long plume of smoke. The explosion rattled doors and windows and sounded like loud thunder.

But that meteor was trifling as compared with a meteorite that fell in Siberia in 1908. Although almost thirty years have passed since the event, *The Advent Witness* (London) reported in 1936:

Airplanes and a staff of scientists are shortly to begin a search for the Tungus meteorite, believed to be the largest meteorite the world has ever known. It fell in the valley of the River Tunguska in Northern Siberia in 1908 and was stated to have devastated an area of eleven thousand square miles. Had it fallen on London the entire city would have been wiped out.. Its fall was accompanied by an earthquake in Siberia. It is hoped that photographs taken from the air when the snow has cleared and the woods are still bare will show both the direction in which the trees fell when swept over by the meteorite's fall and full details of the craters formed by the impact of the meteorite.

In 1936 Dr. Harlow Shapley, Director of Harvard Observatory, reported that it had been "an unusual season for star explosions."

On April 29, 1937, the New York *Times* published the following dispatch:

> The worst magnetic storm in a hundred years has been raging during the past four days in the great ocean of magnetism surrounding the earth, it was reported today at the meeting of the American Geophysical Union by Dr. A. G. McNish of the Department of Terrestial Magnetism, Carnegie Institution of Washington. The magnetic storm, which consists of unusually large fluctuations in the earth's magnetic field, started on Sunday and is still going on. It is being studied at the Magnetic observatory of the Coast and Geodetic Survey at Cheltenham, Md. The deviations of the magnetic needle at the observatory, Dr. McNish said, have been highly erratic and reached as high as seventy minutes, the largest observed in a century. The storm is causing severe interference in communications. Telegraph companies reported "dead" periods, and radio signals have been subjected to sudden and severe fading. The disturbances in the earth's magnetic field, which are believed to be correlated with sun-spot activity, have recently been partly explained by the accumulation of evidence for the existence of mighty rivers of electricity flowing in circular paths around the earth's magnetic poles.

When the late Dr. Jonathan Goforth was in Philadelphia in December, 1935, he told me of a remark made by an astronomer connected with the Mount Wilson Observatory in California, which houses the largest telescope lens in the world. The astronomer said that they dared not make public what they were now seeing in the heavens, of explosions and cataclysmic phenomena, for they feared that if this were given publicity people would be thrown into a panic.

Are not these stupendous and multiplying signs in the skies, as predicted, the near forerunners of the final heavenly cataclysms that shall end this age and accompany the Lord's return in glory? We read of the very end: "And, lo, there was a great earthquake; and the sun became black as sackcloth of hair, and the moon became as blood; and the stars of heaven fell unto the earth, even as a fig tree casteth her untimely figs, when she is shaken of a mighty wind. And the heaven departed as a scroll when it is rolled together" (Rev. 6:12-14). Still later: "And the fourth angel poured out his vial upon the sun; and power was given unto him to scorch men with fire. And men were scorched with great heat, and blasphemed the name of God, which hath power over these plagues: and they repented not to give him glory" (Rev. 16:8, 9).

And then comes the end of the heavenly signs, with the coming of the Sun of righteousness Himself. Immediately after "the powers of heaven shall be shaken" we read: "And then shall they see the Son of man coming in a cloud with power and great glory" (Luke 21:26, 27). "For as the lightning cometh out of the east, and shineth even unto the west; so also shall the coming of the Son of man be" (Matt. 24:27).

XV

THE SIGN OF LAWLESSNESS

LAWLESSNESS as a characteristic of today is a conspicuous sign of the times. The "man of sin," the "son of perdition," who is to be revealed at the very end after the apostasy or "falling away" that is now taking place, is "that Lawless one" (2 Thess. 2:8, marg.) "who opposeth and exalteth himself above all that is called God." Lawlessness sets itself above law, which originates in God. "The last days" are described by the Holy Spirit as "perilous times" when "men shall be"—not lovers of God, or lovers of the law, but—"lovers of their own selves, . . . blasphemers, disobedient to parents, . . . trucebreakers, incontinent, . . . despisers of those that are good, traitors" (2 Tim. 3:1-4). These characteristics all go with lawlessness. Vast numbers of people today, including children, young people, college students, and mature men and women, scoff at law, and glory in ignoring or defying every semblance of law in every walk of life. This widespread, outspoken, unblushing lawlessness has broken out noticeably since the beginning of the World War.

We find lawlessness in art—in music, painting, and literature; lawlessness in morals; lawlessness in government; lawlessness in religion.

In music, for example, as in other forms of art, there is an abandonment and defiance of the principles that make for beauty and truth. All music lovers know that this is so; the so-called "Modern" music is an expression of it. Not only is this lawlessness seen in the baser forms of music today, appealing to the worst in human nature and abandoning all semblance of control, such as "swing music," but it is found even in the symphonic field, recognized and approved by some symphony orchestra leaders of highest standing.

120

The triumph of Fundamentalism in music was set forth in a remarkable article in *The Sunday School Times* (Sept. 29, 1934) by Dr. John B. Nield, a well known Christian organist and choirmaster, describing a piano recital given in Los Angeles by the master pianist of the century, Paderewski. Dr. Nield describes Paderewski's masterly work at the piano that night, his "crashing, reverberating chords and sforzandos," his "marvelous mastery of phrasing, such ethereal shading and delicate traces and limpid scale playing," and then says:

It was a veritable triumph for Fundamentalists (that is, for those who have not overthrown the music of Bach, Mozart, and Händel for the heart-rending cacophonies of the advanced (?) schools of Modernists. What a shock it must have been for any Modernists who were present! There was not a single number on the program that was not of the old-fashioned school. Happily we were saved the sound of the Modernist strainings and groanings of the whole-tone scale (both unnatural and unscientific) with its hideous dissonances and false relations. Yes, we had dissonances, but written and resolved as only the masters knew how to prepare and resolve them, which is a very different matter in their lawful and logical use. The audience "heard gladly" the simple, grand, and well-tried masterpieces of Bach, Liszt, Schubert, and Chopin. In his choice of program, Paderewski brought a new triumph for those who hold dear that which we consider our great heritage musically. His art was a new victory for the old message. Again we were all forcefully reminded that the very survival of these century-old compositions which the master played is in itself enough to justify their having become the standard of measurement in musical literature.

Dr. Nield drew spiritual lessons from that experience, and one was this: "That Christians need to sit at the feet of the Master himself—to learn of him the hidden harmonies, the flowing melody, the sacred touch, the true technique of the art of living."

In painting, the lawlessness of Futuristic and Cubist art, and Surrealism, and similar grotesque expressions, is ridiculed by some, reverenced by others.

In literature there is, by some writers who pride themselves on having discernment and ability, such an abandonment of the canons of strength and beauty and legitimate appeal in writing, that the result is hardly intelligible to a reader of normal mentality.

We are seeing lawlessness in government in various countries today, especially in Russia, Italy, and Germany, where law is frankly abandoned for the whims and dictatorship of one man. That it is a deadly peril in the United States, with powerful forces working insidiously for it, cannot be denied.

Feminism, so-called, shows us woman insisting upon taking her place in any and every vocation, responsibility, and activity of man, and thus it is a plain expression of the lawlessness of humanity today in revolt against God. For God has ordained a distinction between the sexes, in their responsibilities and mutual relationship. Woman cannot take over man's responsibilities and offices, in certain lines of government and rulership, without defying God. But defiance of God is the keynote of today's lawlessness. "As for my people," said God to Israel in prophesied judgment, "children are their oppressors, and women rule over them" (Isa. 3:12). I once asked Miss Christabel Pankhurst, who with her mother had taken such a militant part in securing woman suffrage in Great Britain, how she felt now, since her new vision of Christ's return, about "Votes for Women"? "I am glad we secured the vote," she answered, "if for no other reason than to show that women are just as powerless as men to improve conditions in the world."

In morals, all the old standards—which means God's standards—are being swept away in many circles and openly laughed at. One need only to run through the pages of modern magazines and books coming from some of our "best" publishing houses, to see this. A book published abroad and banned from America in 1929 was adjudged "obscene" in 1932 by the United States Customs Court, then was admitted without restriction in 1934, as announced by the National Council on Freedom from Censorship.

The spiritual condition of some of our churches may be seen from such a news item as this: In a church in the Southwest fifteen pretty dancing girls, wearing pajama suits and long gray silk dresses and with bare feet, danced before a Sunday evening congregation. They "interpreted" such hymns as "My Faith Looks Up to Thee," and "Hark! The Herald Angels Sing." The swaying and gliding of these girls was supposed to symbolize supplication, humility, and prayer. And the president of the Board of Trustees of the church said he was sure that none of the three hundred persons in attendance was unfavorably impressed!

Abandonment of decency in dress by girls and women is evident everywhere, especially on bathing beaches, where lawlessness in behavior as well as in costume is a commonplace. The logical conclusion is Nudism, which has come as a philosophy and cult accepted by many, and defended by still others who do not practice it. As *The Sunday School Times* showed editorially (Nov. 2, 1935), Nudism not only outrages every decent person but is the logical climax of man's revolt against God. For God's Word tells us that the necessity for clothing was a direct result of man's sin in the fall. God provided clothing for Adam and Eve, who became conscious of their nakedness after and because of the fall; and the coats of skins that God made for them, "and clothed them" (Gen. 3:21), were a type of the "covering" or blood atonement of the Son of God, "the Lamb of God, which taketh away the sin of the world" (John 1:29). Thus God forbade nakedness from the time sin entered the human race; and nakedness and clothing are inseparably connected with the facts of sin and redemption.

Lawless man does not like to admit this, "because the carnal mind is enmity against God" (Rom. 8:7). Yet the human race in general has accepted the necessity of clothing; but it remained for the Nudists of these last days to carry the present revolt against God to the lowest depths of obscene blasphemy to which man has yet sunk. "For of this sort are they which creep into houses, and lead captive silly women laden with sins, led away with divers lusts" (2 Tim. 3:6). Another terrible Scripture passage describes much of lawless humanity today:

Them that walk after the flesh in the lust of uncleanness, and despise government. Presumptuous are they, self-willed, they are not afraid to speak evil of dignities. . . . But these, as natural brute beasts, made to be taken and destroyed, speak evil of the things that they understand not; and shall utterly

perish in their own corruption; and shall receive the reward
of unrighteousness, as they that count it pleasure to riot in
the day time.   Spots they are and blemishes, sporting themselves with their own deceivings, while they feast with you;
having eyes full of adultery, and that cannot cease from sin;
beguiling unstable souls: an heart they have exercised with
covetous practices; cursed children. . . . These are wells without water, clouds that are carried with a tempest; to whom
the mist of darkness is reserved for ever (2 Pet. 2:10-17).

Immorality, or lawlessness in morals, is not only toler-
ated but actually approved and recommended to young
people by certain teachers in our schools and colleges.   Such
teachers, writers and "apostles" of what they call "the
new liberty" which is only lawlessness, are described with
photographic accuracy in these inspired words: *"While they
promise them liberty, they themselves are the servants of
corruption"* (2 Pet. 2:19).

Lawlessness is found in the world of science, which prides
itself on the "passion for truth."   The notorious case of
Haeckel is well known.   When Haeckel was convicted by
the faculty of his own university, in his old age, of altering
or doctoring certain animal illustrations designed to sustain
his evolution theories, he made the following statement:

I should feel utterly condemned and annihilated by the
admission *were it not that hundreds of the best observers and
biologists lie under the same charge.*   The great majority of
all morphological, anatomical, histological, embryological dia-
grams are not true to nature, but more or less doctored,
schematized, and reconstructed.

When all these true and decent things go by the board
in the obsession of lawlessness that is destroying the world,
of course character goes.   *Harpers Magazine* published a
remarkable article (August, 1933) by James Truslow
Adams, on "The Crisis in Character."   Mr. Adams discusses the economic crisis and the political crisis, and then
shows that the character crisis is the most serious of all.
He marshals facts that are depressing.   Flabbiness of moral
fiber, he shows, is found in many places where we would
least expect it.   One of the most distinguished news journals, says Mr. Adams, "did not hesitate to publish false
statements about certain happenings in a foreign capital,

. . . and in doing so the paper disregarded the protests of its correspondent on the spot who, like all others who were there, knew the statements to be wholly false." Concerning advertisers, Mr. Adams says: "The character of the American citizen as envisaged by the advertiser is a sorry spectacle of spiritual sordidness; and there is perhaps no other group of business men who know their business so well as do the advertisers."

The author of *Christianity and the Social Crisis* has made this startlingly clear when he says:

We cannot conceal from ourselves that in some directions the temptations of modern life are so virulent that character and reputation are collapsing around us with sickening frequency. The prevalence of fraud and the subtler kinds of dishonesty for which we have invented the new term "graft" is a sinister fact of the greatest import. It is not merely the weak who fall, but the strong, clean, kindly, religious men stoop to methods so tricky, hard and rapacious that we stand aghast whenever the curtain is drawn aside and we are shown the inside facts.

But the chapter of Scripture which describes all this stampede of lawlessness in such vivid detail, 2 Timothy 3, does not leave us blinded and hopeless in these "perilous times." It begins with the warning of danger and ends with the way of safety. "Evil men and seducers shall wax worse and worse," but God's people, like Timothy, are to "continue . . . in the things" which they have learned and been assured of, holding fast to "all scripture," which is "given by inspiration of God," that they may be "throughly furnished unto all good works."

XVI

THE REVOLT OF YOUTH

YOUTH'S insistent domination of life today is one of the signs of the times. It is specially recognized in the prophetic Scriptures, Old Testament as well as New. In the "perilous times" of "the last days" we are told that humanity shall be "disobedient to parents" and "without natural affection" (2 Tim. 3:2, 3). Could there be a more accurate description of the characteristic spirit of many children and young people today? But seven centuries before Paul wrote of the last days, Isaiah made predictions of the same time by inspiration of the same Holy Spirit. He gives a long prophecy introduced by the words, "And it shall come to pass in the last days" (Isa. 2:2). Here is one of the events seen more than two and a half millenniums before it occurs: "The child shall behave himself proudly against the ancient and the base against the honorable" (Isa. 3:5). Just before this the divinely inspired prophet declares for God: "And I will give children to be their princes, and babes shall rule over them."

One evening in October, 1930, the elder statesmen of the British Empire were assembled at a banquet in Guildhall in London, in an Imperial conference. The Dominion Secretary, J. H. Thomas, was in the midst of an address, when a Cambridge undergraduate broke into the meeting, interrupted Mr. Thomas, forced him rudely into a seat and then took the floor, haranguing the assemblage for several minutes before he was ejected. His topic was the modest theme of youth and its capacity to right the wrongs of the world. According to the *Philadelphia Public Ledger* Foreign Service, reporting this incident, the young man explained ruefully, "I was going to ask them to give youth a chance."

The worst of it is that young people today are actually

126

trained, in many homes and schools and colleges, to accept nothing as absolute or final, to experiment for themselves, to give full play to self-expression and do as they want to do. Dan Gilbert writes, in his book, *Our Retreat from Modernism:*

Only a few months ago I happened to be present at the opening of the semester at a State Teachers College. I heard the address of welcome delivered by the President to the incoming freshmen. In part, this is what he said: "Accept absolutely nothing until you have proved it to your own satisfaction. Take nothing on your parents' say-so, or your minister's. The maxims, moral and otherwise, of the alleged 'wise men' of old have no meaning for the present age. Times have changed. What was true yesterday is not true today; what was right yesterday is not right today. Have a modern outlook and a modern mind. Don't let your mind be a storehouse, and your life an outworking, of antique ideas. Don't live by moral standards which are out-of-date; they may have been good once, they aren't now."

And even religious leaders encourage our young people to suppose they can take a place of leadership that God never intended them to have. *The Sunday School Times* published an editorial (July 11, 1936) discussing a shocking exhibit of this. The so called New History Society has as its goal the establishment of the United States of the World and of a Universal Religion. Founded in 1928, it is based on Bahai principles,—and Bahaism, aiming to be a super-religion that welcomes members of every creed, has built a beautiful temple near Lake Michigan at Wilmette, Ill., the architecture being a combination of old Egyptian, Gothic, Arabic, Romanesque, Byzantine, and Renaissance. This New History Society a few years ago offered prizes for the best papers on the subject, "How Can Youth Contribute to the Realization of a Universal Religion?" The judges included Bishop Fred Fisher, Dr. Henry F. Atkinson, General Secretary of the World Conference for International Peace Through Religion, and several Unitarian ministers. Such a competition is good preparation for the universal religion that will head up in, and worship, the Beast and the Antichrist of Revelation.

In the early Nineteen Twenties there was a Youth Movement in Germany which drew from casual American observers glowing reports (as in Stanley High's *Youth Movements*). Inside of five years *Pflugschaar,* its onetime organ, declared that "that which still shows signs of life has but the convulsive twitchings of a dying organism," and the *Reichsbote* commented: "This was to be expected. These youth looked down on their elders and expected to accomplish what their elders were not able to accomplish."

Satan needs young people today as never before. For the Lord's return is near, and Satan knows his time is short. A Bible teacher whose ministry among young people is being greatly blessed says, with keen discernment:

Surely the end of the Gentile age is near, and the Antichrist is marshalling his forces with a grim determination, and all of it seems forced against the young people! Why? Because it is the youths which he shall use in his kingdom. He will not have time, in the brief three and a half years, for the children to grow up, and many of the older ones will prefer martyrdom rather than serve him after they see through his schemes.

Here is a dreadful probability indeed; and we are seeing its beginnings in convincing reality. The Communists and Reds have their diabolical schools for children, in which the youth and little ones are trained to deny, dishonor, and blaspheme God and His Christ, thus becoming ready and eager disciples of Satan. What a challenge, to all of us who know and love Christ as Saviour and Lord, to work and pray as never before to bring the children of this generation to him! Our Lord's words take on a new meaning when He said:

And whoso shall receive one such little child in my name receiveth me. But whoso shall offend one of these little ones which believe in me, it were better for him that a millstone were hanged about his neck, and that he were drowned in the depth of the sea (Matt. 18:5, 6).

XVII

SPIRITISM AND ASTROLOGY

IT IS popular, among many well-educated people today, to dismiss all belief in evil spirits as ignorance and superstition. If this attitude is correct and there are no evil spirits, then the most brilliant and intellectual human leader Christianity has ever had, the apostle Paul, and also the Lord Jesus Christ Himself, were ignorant and superstitious. For Christ and Paul, together with many other parts of the inspired Scriptures, declare unmistakably the fact of evil spirits as well as of good spirits or God's angels. "We wrestle not against flesh and blood," declares Paul, "but against principalities, against powers, against the rulers of the darkness of this world, against spiritual wickedness in high places [the heavenlies]" (Eph. 6:12). Christ repeatedly recognized the existence of Satan and evil spirits, and spoke to them with authority, commanding and for bidding them as He would (John 8:44; Luke 8:26-33; and many other passages).

There is a woe and warning uttered in prophecy in Revelation: "Woe to the inhabiters of the earth and of the sea! for the devil is come down unto you, having great wrath, because he knoweth that he hath but a short time" (Rev. 12:12). The time there predicted has doubtless not come yet, but the fulfillment of so many Scripturally predicted signs of the times points to its speedy approach, and there can be no question that Satan and his hosts of evil spirits are active as never before in the vain hope of defeating Christ and the Church in their final and supreme struggle for the dominion of this earth and of mankind.

There are many evidences of the increasing activities of evil spirits today in the affairs of men. During and since the World War there has been a noticeable revival of Spiritism. The deaths of so many millions of young men in the war, beloved sons and brothers in their family circles, turned countless numbers of their sorrowing relatives to seek comfort and assurance from spirit mediums. This wave of Spiritism is continuing, bringing misery, Satanic bondage, sometimes insanity, and the awful peril of the second death, to its devotees.

God warned Israel against Spiritism, and also the church:

> And when they shall say unto you, Seek unto them that have familiar spirits, and unto wizards that peep, and that mutter: should not a people seek unto their God? for the living to the dead? To the law and to the testimony: if they speak not according to this word, it is because there is no light in them (Isa. 8:19, 20).

Obedience to this command of God, with God's high approval, is recorded of the godly King Josiah of Judah:

> Moreover the workers with familiar spirits, and the wizards, and the images, and the idols, and all the abominations . . . did Josiah put away, that he might perform the words of the law . . . And like unto him was there no king before him, that turned to the Lord with all his heart, and with all his soul, and with all his might (2 Kings 23:24, 25).

There are parts of God's Word that every medium and evil spirit will vehemently or angrily reject—while, of course, they will deceive by using other Scriptures, as do all false cults. Paul warns:

> Now the Spirit speaketh expressly, that in the latter times some shall depart from the faith, giving heed to seducing spirits, and doctrines of devils; speaking lies in hypocrisy; having their conscience seared with a hot iron; forbidding to marry, and commanding to abstain from meats, which God hath created to be received with thanksgiving of them which believe and know the truth (1 Tim. 4:1-3).

It is well known that Spiritist mediums practice vegetarianism.

Not long ago the forty-fourth annual convention of the National Spritualists Association was held, which includes five hundred churches and forty thousand of the two hundred thousand believers of Spiritism in America. A competitive organization is the International General Assembly of Spiritualists, which claims two hundred churches.

A missionary in West Africa writes me that a clairvoyant recently sent a letter and Spiritist literature to one of the natives in the African mission field. The missionary responded by writing a vigorous letter of Scriptural testimony to the medium, warning him and calling his attention to the Scriptures denouncing Spiritism, and to the Lord Jesus as the only Saviour. Spiritism is reaching out after the whole world.

A consecrated Christian husband and wife who are doing a true work of evangelism and Bible teaching in the Northwest write of an amazing experience that illustrates the increase of Spiritist cults. The letter was published in *The Sunday School Times* of April 19, 1936:

> We are working in a Community Church. The pastor preaches a good sermon in the morning, and then turns the evening service over to the enemy, inviting various entertainers, musicians, and apparently anyone who cares to take part.
>
> Last night after the service a psychoanalyst entertained the crowd by crystal-gazing and fortune-telling. He has spent two years in India studying his art, so he is well qualified to "analyze" any who care for it. Just an hour before I had given our young people the fourth chapter in the book, *The Triumph of John and Betty Stam*, and had stressed our need to lay all on the altar and allow Christ to live in us. I have been asked to sponsor the Epworth League, and since last June three of our young people have been saved. But each Sunday evening the opposition is terrific.

In England, professing Christian ministers are showing an ominous interest in Spiritism. *The Advent Witness* (London, April, 1937) publishes this note:

> "Christianity can be saved by spiritualism with the co-operation of the churches." This assertion was made at a gathering of clergymen and ministers in Leeds, arranged by the Confraternity of Spiritualists, Clergy, and Ministers to discuss closer relations between Christianity and psychic research. The Rev. G. M. Elliott, who gave up a living at Cricklewood to devote his time to the work of the Confraternity, told how he and a well-known dean approached the Archbishop of York and urged that the Church of England should carry out a thorough investigation of spiritualism. "To my amazement and intense

delight," went on Mr. Elliott, "the Archbishop agreed and told us a commission must be appointed. That commission has been appointed and the dean who was with me is its chairman."

Mr. Panton, Editor of *The Dawn* (London) has called attention to the fact that Spiritism may be called the art of waking wood. Sir Oliver Lodge is quoted: "A light table seems no longer inert; it behaves as if animated. It can exhibit certainty, it can seek for information, it can convey it." Mr. Panton continues: "Here is a fact which is a thrilling comment. Mr. J. Vine Milne writes (*Outlook*, Jan. 30, 1920): 'I had been spending an evening with a friend, an M.A. and D.Sc. of London. It was not long before we heard knocks, which we spelt out aloud. It was a reference to Habakkuk. We eagerly turned up the passage, which read: "Woe unto him that saith *to the wood*, Awake; to the *dumb stone*, Arise; it shall teach" (Hab. 2:19). A great silence fell on us. I took it as a personal warning, and this was forty years ago: I have not touched the unclean thing since.'"

Astrology is having a great revival. It is coming to the front again with other Satanic movements, and will probably have increasing influence over all classes of men, the most intellectual as well as the ignorant, until the Lord comes. Leading newspapers and magazines have their regular departments in which astrologers give advice; national leaders in various countries are said to take no important step today without first consulting an astrologer; the teachings of astrologers are even coming over the radio through the air—and "the prince of the power of the air" must welcome this.

The Advent Witness comments on a book published in 1927 by a well known astrologer who called himself Cheiro, which contained the prediction: "Viewing the future I see great and menacing times overshadowing England, while over the Palace of King George and the Royal Family the immediate present and the coming years are full of ominous signs that have no parallel in recent times." There followed a penetrating study of the (then) Prince of Wales, with this statement: "It is well within the range of possibility . . . that he will fall a victim of a devastating love affair. If he does, I predict that the Prince will give up everything, even the chance of being crowned, rather than lose the object of his affection." Satan can doubtless make some correct predictions, but God warned His people long ago that, if a prophet should foretell a sign or a wonder that should come to pass, they must not "hearken unto the words of that prophet" if his message was, "Let us go after other gods" (Deut. 13:1-3).

Astrology makes much of studying the positions and movements of the stars and then directing our actions in accordance with such times as the stars indicate. Manasseh, king of Judah, "did that which was evil in the sight of the Lord, after the abominations of the heathen," for he "observed times, and used enchantments, and dealt with familiar spirits" (2 Kings 21:6). But God's law plainly forbade this. "Ye shall not . . . use enchantment, nor observe times" (Lev. 19:26). This warning was repeated in Deuteronomy 18:10. The child of God never needs to consult spirits or stars for guidance as to times; he has the Holy Spirit as his infallible guide, and his song is: "I trusted in thee, O Lord: I said, Thou art my God. My times are in thy hand" (Psa. 31:14, 15).

Of Manasseh, one of Judah's most corrupt kings, who made God's people "to do worse than the heathen" (2 Chron. 33:9), we read that he "worshiped all the host of heaven, and served them" (2 Kings 21:3). But when Josiah came to the throne he burned "all the vessels that were made . . . for all the host of heaven," and he cast out "the idolatrous priests . . . that burned incense unto Baal, to the sun, and to the moon, and to the planets, and to all the host of heaven" (2 Kings 23:4, 5). When men today subject their lives and actions to the movements of the stars, is it not a form of worship?

Collier's magazine, in its department "Keep Up with the World," by Freling Foster, notes: "Despite the fact that astrology has been ridiculed by intelligent people and even banned by law in many countries for 4,800 years, it remains today the most elaborately organized of all superstitions. In the United States, astrologers still are licensed to forecast future events."

A full-page newspaper article in December, 1936, widely circulated, discussed "Astonishing Predictions for the Year

1937," and gave the forecasts of prominent astrologers. It said that the mantle of astrologer Evangeline Adams had fallen upon Myra Kingsley, who predicted that the United States this year was in for a wave of prosperity. Prosperity has not largely materialized—perhaps the stars overlooked the strikes! Nella Webb, "another of New York's outstanding prognosticators," declared that the stars in their courses showed that there would probably be a delay with the Coronation. But the Coronation was held on time.

God's prophecies never fail. But evil spirits are misleading men, and men are exalting man—just as God said they would.

XVIII

THE REVOLT AGAINST GOD AND HIS SON

WHILE the spirit of revolt against God is expressed in many different ways today, there are certain outstanding manifestations of this revolt which fulfill, in sinister detail and with startling accuracy, the Second Psalm: "The kings of the earth set themselves, and the rulers take counsel together, against the Lord, and against his anointed, saying, Let us break their bands asunder, and cast away their cords from us." Soviet Russia and Germany are the two nations fulfilling this prophetic picture.

A Russian university in Leningrad is reported to have been opened to "teach atheism." Its three hundred students, of whom forty-seven are women, will prepare themselves for "active propaganda of militant atheism." The comment has been made: "It suggests a colony of ants on a railroad right-of-way organizing a university to prove that there is no such thing as an engineer."

The Dawn (London) says: "The personal and open hate of Christ, than which nothing could be more diabolic, grows amazingly, and ought to warn the Church that the hour is late. The Internationale of Free Thinkers, which operates outside Russia, has as its emblem an athlete straining to smash the cross upon which the Crucified is nailed head downward." *The Bible for China*, February, 1933, reports: "Russian children wear blasphemous pictures of Christ in cheap shoes. They carry clubs picturing Christ as a demon. The stores display pictures of Christ below which is written, 'See me as I am'; and on the other side is a picture of the Devil." Again, it is reported that

The Soviet Publishing Trust recently was compelled to destroy 200,000 copies of a new edition of a book written by the Russian poet Alexander Pushkin. The proofreader had overlooked the word "God" (printed even with a capital G) and all books of the edition had to be ground up as soon as they came from the press. The Soviet has issued a handbook entitled, *What Shall I Do in Case My Parents Try to Force Me to Go to Church?* The advice given includes the following: Report the case to the authorities; call the police, bring action before the courts. The punishment is loss of work, starvation and death. Lenin's summary (*On Religion*, p. 50) is: "All religious ideas are an unspeakable abomination."

The atheism of Communism is not confined to Russia but is reaching out into the whole world. Communist Sunday schools, as many as one hundred and twenty-four, are said to have been established in England, and in their catechism are the following questions and answers:

What is God? God is a word used to designate an imaginary being which people of themselves have devised.

Who is Jesus Christ? Jesus Christ is the son of a Jewish girl named Mary.

Is he the Son of God? There is no God, therefore there can be no God's Son.

Is Christianity desirable? Christianity is not advantageous to us, but it is harmful, it makes spiritual cripples. By its teaching of bliss after death it deceives the people. Christianity is the greatest obstacle to the progress of mankind, therefore it is the duty of every citizen to help to wipe out Christianity.

It is impressively significant that Bible prophecy is unconsciously fulfilled by leaders of the anti-God revolt. *The King's Business* has reported:

Recently the Soviet Government issued a special and most significant postage stamp. It was issued to commemorate the tenth anniversary of the Red Army's cavalry. The flag carried by the leading horseman is blood red—the flag of Russia's Red Army and the emblem of World Communism. The line apparently marking the pathways is likewise red on the original stamp —the red pathway of Gog. The designer of this stamp probably never read a line of the Apocalypse. Yet who, familiar with the Bible, can look upon this stamp and fail to think of the four famous horsemen of Revelation 6, starting forth on their ride to judgment and to death? These appear to be setting the world afire as they ride. Note the Sea of Azov. They seem to be heading toward Palestine. Did God guide the hands of Gog's workman in the making of this stamp, to the end that it should speak to those who have ears to hear in these momentous hours? If these ride forth to the mountains of Israel, they will ride forth never to return!

What will the end be? The Second Psalm, predicting the revolt that we are now seeing, predicts also the end. "He that sitteth in the heavens shall laugh: the Lord shall have them in derision. Then shall he speak unto them in his wrath, and vex them in his sore displeasure." A fearful glimpse of the ultimate has perhaps already been given to us in the alleged report of a Captain Francis McCullagh, an eye-witness of the trial of Roman priests in Moscow: "On the night after the archbishop and his companions were paraded in a motor-lorry through the streets of Moscow, the terrible leader of the Reds gazed in horror on one more terrible than himself, on a dread, nocturnal visitor who, having passed swiftly through the triple guards and the bolted doors, had halted at his bedside and laid an icy hand on the proud and formidable brain. From that day Lenin was a living corpse." Percival Phillips gives the rumor than ran through all Russia on Lenin's death (*Daily Mail*, Feb. 1, 1924): "The once all-powerful Dictator of Red Russia spent his last days of activity crawling on all fours like a beast around the room in his carefully-guarded retreat at Gorky, apologizing to the furniture for his misdeeds—the memory of which remained amid the ruins of his mind—and shouting repeatedly, 'God save Russia and kill the Jews!' "

Germany has followed on after Russia in the revolt against God. Although their political systems are sharply opposed to each other, Communism, Nazism and Fascism have certain things in common: dictatorship, the destruction of personal liberty, and in varying degrees the rejection of the authority of God.

True Christians must travel a thorny and dangerous pathway in Germany. The newspapers carry frequent cabled dispatches reporting the Nazis' determined purpose "to reform the Christian Church," which means to destroy it. Back in April, 1933, the *Public Ledger* Foreign Service reported:

The Hitler revolution entered a new and immensely significant phase today when 39,000,000 Christians in the German Federation Evangelical Church learned that the National Socialists propose to discharge many of their pastors and to reorganize the constitution of the Church to eliminate its democratic forms, to exclude leaders not in agreement with National Socialism, and to rebuild the ecclesiastical structure of Protestant Germany on the basis of Hitler patriotism, nationalism, and "purity of race." . . . Christ himself was a Hitlerite, the assembly was informed by the pastor, Dr. Wieneke of Soldin, who declared: "The Christian cross and the swastika belong together. Under these two emblems our theology must be resurrected."

Two years later, in August, 1935, the Philadelphia *Record* published an interview with Professor Wilhelm Hauer, leader of the German pagans. Said he: "We must have buildings, yes. But we are counting on getting possession of plenty of Christian churches." The reporter, an American pastor, commented: "In Russia many church buildings now serve as atheistic museums. In Germany a powerful and growing heathen cult visualizes the extinction of Christianity. Already the pagans are planning to move into the Christian houses of worship." Gericke, head of the pagan movement in Berlin, said: "Christianity has failed too completely."

This American pastor-reporter had a long conversation with a young university student who claimed to be a loyal pagan, and who labored to explain why German youth must and would turn from Christianity to paganism. "During our whole conversation the German student did not mention the word God. On the whole, the Christian conception of personal Deity is meaningless to the German pagans. In conversation with me Professor Hauer used the word God, and then added, 'If I may use that expression.'" It is the conviction of this American pastor that for several millions of Germans the Nazi party has become a creed and a religion, and that for all such "Hitler has supplanted Christ as the object of supreme allegiance."

The *Literary Digest* (April 22, 1933), published an extended article on "Making a German Christ for Germany." It stated that:

German Nazis are nailing the swastika to the cross to make an Aryan Church. All traces of the Jewish ancestry of the Christian faith are to be removed by making Christ a German, and by substituting German mythology for the Old Testament. Thor and Wotan will be substituted for Moses and Isaiah, and tribal sagas will take the place of Proverbs and Solomon's Songs. Jews may not enter the new sanctuary, and those who marry Jews will be excommunicated. . . . This effort to capture the Church for the Nazis is undertaken by a group known as the "German Christians," who held their first federal conference in 1933. Strong resolutions adopted asked for "equal fusion of the Church with the Nazi movement in a pure Aryan spirit; . . . dismissal of the Old Testament basis, and substitution of the German inheritance; instead of prophets, sagas and fairy-tales to take the leading personalities from German spiritual, philosophical, and artistic life."

What a fulfillment of prophecy this is! "For the time will come when they will not endure sound doctrine; but after their own lusts shall they heap to themselves teachers, having itching ears; and they shall turn away their ears from the truth, and shall be turned unto fables (2 Tim. 4:3, 4).

But the hopeful side of the picture is that there are millions of true Christians in Germany, who undoubtedly would lay down their lives before they would accept this pagan, anti-God and anti-Christ position. Naming various Protestant denominations, the *Literary Digest* says that "all these Christians are opposed to the Nazi program." They desire "the maintenance of the entire body of the Christian faith, including the Old Testament. The substitution of profane sagas is unthinkable."

In April, 1936, an Associated Press dispatch reported an adaptation of the Sermon on the Mount to the German viewpoint by Reichsbischof Ludwig Mueller, the main feature of which is the elimination of all reference to Jerusalem, King Solomon, Pharisees, the scribes, laws and prophets, and the Ten Commandments. These references, although in Matthew's Gospel, were held to be Jewish and therefore must be rejected.

A magazine article entitled "Hitler Has Changed the Bible," says that "The Jesus who goose-steps through the pages of Realmbishop Mueller addressed himself not to all men but primarily, if not solely, to Mueller's racial com-patriots. The figure that emerges is no longer Jesus of Nazareth but Jesus of Naziland." Matthew 5:21, says this article, is the crucial test: how will Mueller meet it? The Scripture reads: "Ye have heard that it was said by them of old time, Thou shalt not kill; and whosoever shall kill shall be in danger of the judgment." This has been revised by Hitler's Mueller: *"You shall not commit assassination; such a murderer is guilty and must be condemned to death."*

A press dispatch from Berlin (Dec. 1936) reported a statement made by Leader Schulz of Pomerania in one of the new castles erected as training schools for future Nazi leaders. "I don't want to be guilty of blasphemy, but I ask you, who was greater, Christ or Hitler? Christ at the time of his death had twelve disciples, who weren't even completely faithful to him. Hitler today has a people of 70,000,000 behind him. We cannot submit to having dif-ferences existing alongside of us which breathe a different spirit from ours. Hence National Socialism claims in all earnestness: 'I am the Lord thy God; thou shalt have no other gods beside me.'" At the same meeting another German leader said: "Christianity is the only enemy of National Socialism and of its reconstructive work among our people."

A teacher in a public school in a Berlin suburb made before his class such a blasphemous statement that it can-not be printed here. Indeed, the newspaper report says that this utterance aroused such protest among the parents of the district that the teacher had to be transferred to another district.

Another dispatch from Berlin (Nov., 1936) reports a demand that the Bible be rewritten, "and particularly that Moses should not be mentioned as the one who received the Ten Commandments." The *Evangelical Christian* (Toronto) in an editorial commenting on this reminds us that Germany led the way years ago in the destructive Higher Criticism of the Bible, and says: "But one trembles to think of the end of the road this once great nation is traveling. History seems to have no meaning for them. Blindly they rush to their own destruction against the thick bosses of the bucklers of Almighty God." This is a reference to Job 15, where we read of "the wicked man": "For he stretcheth out his hand against God, and strengtheneth himself against the Almighty. He runneth upon him, even on his neck, upon the thick bosses of his bucklers."

In December, 1936, an Associated Press dispatch from Berlin reported a series of startling laws promulgated by the Nazi government, one of which is: "Incorporation of every German boy and girl, without exception, into the Hitler Youth Movement, to be trained physically, spiritually and morally."

Back in February, 1934, Hitler's unbridled sovereignty was expressed, according to the Associated Press, when "in a ceremony equal in pomp to an ancient Roman triumph more than a million Nazis throughout the Reich swore obedience to him personally." A blare of trumpets announced the arrival of his personal representative who presided at the ceremony. "The whole realm was connected with Munich by radio. Exactly at the announced moment, 10:30 A.M., leaders of the manifold Nazi organizations stepped forward and joined with thousands of other subleaders assembled before other radios in repeating the following: 'I swear unshakable fidelity to Adolf Hitler, and unquestioning obedience to him and the leaders designated for me by him.'" This oath marked the fourteenth anniversary of the founding of the Nazi party.

The revolt against God includes, of course, a deadly anti-Semitism. In October, 1936, Hitler's personal friend, Julius Steicher, made an epochal address, most of which the *Evangelical Christian* says is unprintable. It quotes from his speech: "If all Jews throughout the world were to be slain in a single night it would be the holiest festive day in the entire history of the world."

A German theologian declares: "The field-grey soldier who throws his last hand-grenade; the dying seaman who, felled by a murderer's hand, pronounces the Fuehrer's (Hitler's) name as his last word—these are for us divine figures much more than is the crucified Jew."

In January, 1937, the German Neo-Paganist general, Von Ludendorff, according to an Associated Press dispatch expressed the Neo-Paganist viewpoint: "We call the Bible what it is—a deceptive work of man for Jews, Rome, and an ambitious priesthood." This dispatch said that the Germanic Faith Movement is trying to suppress the Bible and draw Christians of all faiths from the Church. Bishop Weidemann of Bremen asserted that Christ was not a Jew, and referred to him as "the first great opponent of the Jews."

And now comes a strategic, subtle, but amazingly sinister move by German leadership. Instead of a swift destruction of Christianity there is to be a gradual "evolution" and "absorption" of the old faith. The *Los Angeles Times* of July 19, 1937, publishes a cable from Munich (copyright, 1937, by the *New York Times*), as follows:

Dr. Alfred Rosenberg, who has been described as the supreme pontiff of German neopaganism, has disclosed that the National Socialist church policy aims at the slow but steady absorption of Christianity. He declares that this absorption will crystallize in a situation where "patriotism and religion are one and the same, the service of the Fatherland is divine service and he who loves Germany loves God."

This revelation is contained in a recently issued secret "encyclical" letter dealing with the current struggle between the Catholic Church and the Nazi state. It is marked "strictly confidential for the highest leaders only."

The new Germanic faith of which he is the prophet, Dr. Rosenberg declares, could never have become the country's official religion overnight, and instead of a "frontal attack" a slow but steady evolution was decided upon.

Individual actions like the severance of their church connections by some of the lesser Nazi leaders and the renunciation of Christianity by Hitler's bodyguard were discouraged and forbidden.

It became necessary, Dr. Rosenberg says, to eliminate certain lesser prophets because they entered into direct competition with Christianity when its complete absorption was the aim.

That is why, Dr. Rosenberg explains, although the introduction of a National Socialist religion was decided upon, neither Hitler, Dr. Joseph Goebbels, the Minister of Propaganda, nor any other important Nazi leader renounced, nor will renounce, his formal affiliation with Christianity.

So "he who loves Germany loves God." There is the subtle, lying "recognition" of God, which is in reality the revolt against God and His Son. They pretend also to "recognize" Christ—only He must be "the modern Christ—a tall, lean, strong, light-haired Nordic fighter."

These outspoken national and governmental attacks on God and Christ and the Bible are an ominous fulfillment of prophecy. They will increase until the crucial conflict between Satan-led men and Christ at Armageddon (Rev. 19:11-21). Until then, it is a comfort to remember that Paul wrote by inspiration about the true Church of Christ and those who set themselves against Christ and the written Word of God:

Yea, and all that will live godly in Christ Jesus shall suffer persecution. But evil men and seducers shall wax worse and worse, deceiving, and being deceived. But continue thou in the things which thou hast learned and hast been assured of, knowing of whom thou hast learned them; and that from a child thou hast known the holy scriptures, which are able to make thee wise unto salvation through faith which is in Christ Jesus. All scripture is given by inspiration of God, and is profitable for doctrine, for reproof, for correction, for instruction in righteousness: that the man of God may be perfect, throughly furnished unto all good works (2 Tim. 3:12-17).

XIX

FALSE CHRISTS, AND THE UNPARDONABLE SIN

A PROPHETIC warning of vast significance from the lips of our Lord is this:

Then if any man shall say unto you, Lo, here is Christ, or there; believe it not. For there shall arise false Christs, and false prophets, and shall shew great signs and wonders; insomuch that, if it were possible, they shall deceive the very elect. Behold, I have told you before. Wherefore if they shall say unto you, Behold, he is in the desert; go not forth: behold, he is in the secret chambers; believe it not. For as the lightning cometh out of the east, and shineth even unto the west; so shall also the coming of the Son of man be (Matt. 24:23-27).

This prophecy of false Christs has been having, and continues to have, its fulfillment. Jiddu Krishnamurti, called by *Time* a "doe-eyed Brahman-born Hindu," was announced by Theosophist leaders in 1909, when he was twelve years old, as "the Vehicle of the new World Teacher, the Lord Maitreya," the last preceding coronation of whom on earth was, they said, Jesus Christ. Annie Besant and Charles Leadbeater, Theosophists, trained the boy and young man for his mission, and he became head of their Order of the Star in the East. Apparently he had a large following, but in 1929 Krishnamurti renounced his Messiahship, while still continuing to be a Theosophist seer.

A few years ago a Consolidated Press Association news dispatch from Manila, Philippine Islands, reported:

Every now and then the courts have to deal with a bogus Saviour who has filled his purse among the credulous peasants. Laure Solar has just been sent to prison for eight years and ordered to pay back nine thousand dollars he gathered as he preached in the highways and byways of the village of Capalonga, North Camarines, Island of Luzon. He appeared in

Capalonga with twelve followers, simulating Christ and the apostles. He said that the end of the world was at hand, that Capalonga would be destroyed, but that by paying enough the peasants could be saved by his divine intercession with God. So the folk of Capalonga came through with nine thousand dollars in money and jewels. But just when the collecting was good, the constabulary got on the job and a prosecuting attorney brought criminal charges on which they were convicted.

I verified the authenticity of this item by correspondence with its author, Walter Robb, editor of the *American Chamber of Commerce Journal* at Manila.

Then there is the notorious Negro in Harlem, New York, known as Father Divine, making or permitting the blasphemous claim for himself that he is God. Will Irwin, the well known journalist and editor, has written about him and says that his cult, claiming 20,000,000 adherents, several years ago "was spreading underground through the whole world and was crossing the barrier between his own Negro race and the whites and yellows." On the Pacific Coast it even claims more white followers than Negro. Irwin heard the congregation in this Negro's "Heaven" in Harlem sing a blasphemous adaptation of the Christian hymn "Coronation," using it in worship of the Negro. He heard members of the congregation that day ejaculate: "Father Divine, we know that you are God." To be sure, "Father Divine" was under arrest a few months ago, and put behind the bars. In August, 1937, his lawyer said: "He figures he's too soon for this world and is going to evaporate and return again, perhaps in 1900 years." It seems unbelievable that such a man, or that any man, could be taken seriously today by cultured, intelligent people as well as by the ignorant, when claiming to be Deity,—but God's Word predicts just such "unbelievable" gullibility of those who reject God. Prophecy is being fulfilled.

The *Los Angeles Times* (July 20, 1937) reports:

John Wuest Hunt, self-styled Jesus the Christ, sentenced to three years in Federal prison for violation of the Mann Act (making fornication under certain circumstances a criminal offense), was manacled to a deputy United States Marshal yesterday at the Hall of Justice when he left for McNeil Island.

"I've gained weight here in jail," beamed the rotund follower of Father Divine. "My size 17 collar is a half size too small. I feel fine and am looking forward to my arrival at McNeil Prison."

Hunt, who now weighs more than his normal 220 pounds, was convicted of having transported seventeen-year-old Delight Jewett from her Denver home to Beverly Hills for immoral purposes, convincing her that she was to be a second Virgin Mary destined to bring into the world a new Redeemer.

"I have a book to write while I'm in prison," said Hunt, who plans to ask for a parole at the end of a year in Federal prison. "The name of it is to be *A Little Child Shall Lead Them*. It's to include everything and will be a beautiful thing."

Even Hitler is given a place in such blasphemous claims by his followers. Herr Engelke, a Nazi "Christian," is reported to have said in a lecture:

Christ is not the Son of God in the Biblical sense. God made himself manifest to us in Him as He did in Adolf Hitler. We must give up the Old Testament. Paul and John must recede into the background. We have to destroy everything in order that God may create all anew again.

Alois Spaniol, a Nazi leader, is quoted as having said: "Hitler is a new, a greater, and a more powerful Jesus Christ."

Blasphemy against the Holy Ghost is beginning to appear publicly. Is not this the most ominous sign of all? Several times in the last dozen years I have noted in magazine articles or elsewhere printed statements against the Holy Spirit that I had never seen or heard of before this time.

The Forum magazine published in May, 1928, an article by no less a man than Henry Pratt Fairchild, Professor of Sociology in New York University, entitled "Science in the Trinity." Professor Fairchild modestly proposes as the thesis of his article, which he sets out to prove, that "the Holy Spirit, the Third Person of the Trinity, *is* Science." He says he supports his contention "exclusively by reference to Christ's own words," and he quotes passages from John 14 and 16 in which our Lord said He would send "another Comforter . . . even the Spirit of truth," and that "when he, the Spirit of truth, is come, he will guide you into all truth." Professor Fairchild discusses these passages, and says: "Consider further that Jesus said that this Holy Spirit 'shall teach you all things,' 'will guide you into all truth,' 'will show you things to come.' Could there be a more concise and comprehensive characterization of Science in three brief sentences?" Professor Fairchild does not explain why, if science is really the Holy Spirit, the Third Person of the Trinity, this Deity has led scientists into such an amazing and consistent succession of blunders through the centuries, and through this present generation, and through the past decade. For science and scientists repudiate the findings of science every few years—a fact which scientists constantly recognize and declare. The science of today will be on the scrap heap tomorrow—is it, then, really the work of the Spirit of truth? As some one has said, men seem ready to believe everything but the Bible!

Dr. Kerrl, Chairman of the Prussian Diet, is reported as having said, "Adolf Hitler is the real Holy Ghost."

A leading magazine publishes a review of a book by Aldous Huxley and makes the cheaply flippant comment: "He accuses Swift of the modern sin against the Holy Ghost, sentimentality."

Another widely read magazine publishes a bitter attack on the Christian Church by a well known Southern editor, who tells how he joined the Church as a boy and was disappointed. Describing how he "went to the mourners' bench and professed religion," he says: "I expected to be seized by the Holy Ghost. But I wasn't seized."

One of the most widely read metropolitan newspapers in America publishes an article by a popular "philosopher," whose books are among the best sellers. In ignorant unbelief he attempts to describe the present day. With a garbled knowledge of the New Testament and of Christian history he writes: "This, then, is the meaning of the Age of the Holy Ghost, as opposed to the Age of the Son. After the Age when only belief in the Saviour could bring salvation, there would come another age, more mature, when every man who had attained to a certain level would be able to work out his own salvation." Without any need of belief in Christ today, according to this "philosopher," "the individual, master of himself, freed from the bonds of tradition, begins to realize for himself" all needed truth, and this experience is—realizing the Holy Ghost!

How blind to the truth of the Scriptures is such an interpreter! For the mission of the Holy Ghost is to convict men of sin and show them the Lord Jesus Christ as their only Saviour. "He shall glorify me," said Christ of the Holy Spirit (John 16:14). "No man can say that Jesus is the Lord, but by the Holy Ghost" (1 Cor. 12:3). "We are sanctified through the offering of the body of Jesus Christ once for all . . . Whereof the Holy Ghost also is a witness to us" (Heb. 10:10, 15).

A news sheet or bulletin issued some years ago by the American Association for the Advancement of Atheism published a "joke" about the Holy Spirit that was so blasphemously obscene that it is strange that it was permitted to use the United States mails. But it was fulfilling the prophecy of the Book it vainly hopes to destroy.

It would seem that we are perilously near a time when there may be, as a common thing among men, that overt blasphemy which Christ says cannot be forgiven. Here are His solemn words:

All manner of sin and blasphemy shall be forgiven unto men: but the blasphemy against the Holy Ghost shall not be forgiven unto men. And whosoever speaketh a word against the Son of man, it shall be forgiven him: but whosoever speaketh against the Holy Ghost, it shall not be forgiven him, neither in this world, neither in the world to come (Matt. 12:31, 32).

XX

SUICIDES — AND THE END OF THE AGE

IS SUICIDE a sign of the times? It would seem so. One can hardly pick up a newspaper today without reading of new suicides. The statistics of suicides in Europe indicate that they are far more numerous there than in America—and the suicides in "Christian America" are appalling. Nor are they confined to the ignorant and the poor; constantly they occur among the intellectual, highly educated, well-to-do. The tragedy of it is that suicide is logical for those "having no hope, and without God in the world" (Eph. 2:12). From their premises, believing in no God and no future, why should such hopeless souls continue to incur the misery and hopelessness that have closed in upon them in this world?

An Associated Press dispatch from Warsaw reported that passengers arriving on trains from Moscow and Leningrad said that suicides there in the previous two weeks, during the investigation of the assassination of Sergei Kiroff, had totaled more than four hundred.

The front page of the Philadelphia *Inquirer* reported in May, 1937, the suicide by hanging of a brilliant Haverford College freshman, one of the best minds in his class. It revived memories of a "rumored suicide club" at that college eight years before, when the son of a Superior Court Judge shot himself on the eve of his graduation, and a short time later another student committed suicide.

In 1935 American newspaper readers were shocked when they learned of the suicide of the noted poetess and social worker, Charlotte Perkins Gilman. This seventy-five-year-old genius left a note saying: "When all usefulness is over, when one is assured of an unavoidable and imminent death, it is the simplest of human rights to choose a quick and

149

easy death in place of a slow and horrible one . . . I have preferred chloroform to cancer."

A millionaire, founder and head of one of the best known and most successful business corporations in America, committed suicide a few years ago in his old age. He had all that the world could give him—money, comfort, luxury, success—but, if he had no Christian faith, why—from his hopeless reasoning—should he live on?

A young San Francisco physician, twenty-nine years old, gave himself a hypodermic injection in his arm, stabbed an artery with a knife blade, and slashed his wrists with a razor—and thus "went out." To what? God's Word tells us.

A girl of fourteen in Los Angeles collapsed and died half a block from her home, and it was found that she had taken poison.

The Prophetic News calls attention to the suicides of unconverted Jews:

> The Jews, in view of their commanding position in financial, commercial, and business undertakings, are in a good position to know not only what is going on around them, but what is likely to take place; and when they see that in spite of all their ability, foresight, and riches, they cannot prevent what is coming upon the earth, their hearts fail them for fear. One of the many suicides in this country, where men are daily shooting, drowning, and poisoning themselves, left a letter for a coroner to read. He read it in open court, adding this comment: "This letter was written by an obviously exceptional and intelligent man. If what he writes is true, then the world is in for a very bad time indeed."

One of the most tragic of suicides in many years was that of a family of three, in 1932. The father and mother had been leaders and active in Sunday school work in a foreign mission field and were personal friends of Mrs. Trumbull and myself, having entertained us most hospitably and graciously when we were in the Far East. The tragedy was reported in the papers and in *Time* magazine. Their son had done wrong, and he, with his father and mother, were found seated in an automobile, hands clasped, in a tightly closed garage while the engine had been kept running to generate the deadly carbon monoxide gas. All doubt as to its being suicide was dispelled by the note they had left, reading: "This way accords with our peculiar ideas in cases where conditions warrant it." Although Sunday school workers, they had been conspicuous for their Modernist or Unitarian views.

The Book of Revelation throws light on suicide at the end of the age in this remarkable prophecy: "And in those days shall men seek death, and shall not find it; and shall desire to die, and death shall flee from them" (Rev. 9:6). This points to the prevalence of suicide before that actual prophecy is fulfilled; then, evidently, God in His sovereign power will prevent men from committing suicide although they may do everything in their power to bring it to pass.

Men seeking death, while God longs to give them life! Is it not the story of man and God, from Genesis to Revelation, from the beginning to the end? In Eden man turned away from the life that God had given him, and chose death, as Satan lied to Eve in the temptation to do what God had forbidden, uttering the false prophecy, "Ye shall not surely die" (Gen. 3:4). Satan's prophecy was a lie; God's prophecy was the truth: "in the day that thou eatest thereof thou shalt surely die" (Gen. 2:17). Adam and Eve died spiritually in the day of their disobedience, and later they died physically; but God had provided a Saviour and Redeemer in "the Lamb slain from the foundation of the world" (Rev. 13:8). That Saviour came in His first advent to pay the penalty of man's sin, that all who believe in Him might not die but live. He is coming the second time to complete His redemption of all who are saved and of all creation (Rom. 8:18-23). But He has told us plainly that, as His Second Coming draws nearer, mankind will turn more and more against Him; and we are seeing this prophecy fulfilled.

Mr. Moody used to say that Dr. W. J. Erdman knew the Bible better than any other man in America. I had the privilege of knowing Dr. Erdman intimately, and of learning from him in Scriptural matters, and I have treasured for many years a sentence he wrote me on his eighty-eighth birthday (April 28, 1922). This is what he said: "It is remarkable that the two characteristics of the saints in the Book of the Revelation are their adherence to the

Word of God and the testimony of Jesus they bore—the very two truths denied and assailed in these days."

Many of the most brilliant human intellects today are set implacably against God and Christ. The brilliant Irish philosopher and cynic, Bernard Shaw, addressing the students of Cambridge University, says: "It is a disgrace that in England we have no religion of our own, but we make shift with the discarded legends of the East. Whoever holds that Christ is the Highest possible is a hopeless pessimist, and is not worth working with." And Shaw has also said (*Daily Sketch,* Dec. 1, 1932): "It is high time that we got rid of Jehovah. When the question is raised whether our children shall compound for their sins by sheltering themselves behind Another's sacrifice, whoever hesitates to bring down the knobkerrie [that is, to persecute] is ludicrously unfit to have any part in the government in a modern state." The comment is made: "State persecution of the Christian faith is thus openly advocated by a leading figure of the British Empire for the first time in the modern age."

The Written Word and the Incarnate Word—cultured, intellectual men and women are turning against these two precious, vital, and eternal expressions of God's provision for our life and salvation. *Collier's Magazine* said recently:

Other crises have crowded into the background one of the most significant movements of modern times—the growing attempt to crush Christianity. Today the governments of countries which contain over a third of all Christians are waging a ruthless war against the Christian Church.

Many men hate God's Word—but many love it. It would be a dark world indeed if there were no Bibles. A news item has recently been published that is both alarming and reassuring. It is stated that in a six-hundred room hotel in a certain city the Gideon Bibles were removed at the suggestion of an atheist society. This is of sinister significance,—that atheists should ask for this in Christian America, and that a hotel should comply with their request. But here is the encouragement: the first night after the Bibles were removed more than two hundred inquiries were received as to where the Bibles could be found. The management wisely decided to put the Bibles back in the rooms. While the darkness of the world deepens, the light from above grows brighter. Ralph Norton, of beloved memory, used to express his conviction that the time would come when it would be difficult, if not impossible, to get access to the Word of God or to circulate it freely, because of God's prophetic warning: "Behold, the days come, saith the Lord God, that I will send a famine in the land, not a famine of bread, nor a thirst for water, but of hearing the words of the Lord" (Amos 8:11). Until that day comes should·we not be far more faithful than we have yet been in giving the Word of life freely to all men?

But the dreadful, tragic events and movements that are multiplying on every side must be brought to an end, if humanity is to survive. How can they be ended and the world be saved? Dr. James M. Gray used to quote the words of a godly Harvard graduate, Edward C. Porter: "God will end this age. Men would never end it, any more than a thief would stop stealing." Our hope is in God, not in man.

And there is another reason for the ending of this age by the Lord's return. When the world last looked on Christ, it "derided him, saying, He saved others; let him save himself, if he be Christ, the chosen of God." There was a contemptuous, unbelieving "if" on the lips of the world then. Is that the closing scene in the world's vision of Christ? Christabel Pankhurst calls attention to God's answer when she says that among the reasons for the Lord's return in personal, visible, bodily presence to the earth is this:

The heart of God the Father cannot be satisfied that the world's last sight of His Son shall be that of a persecuted, insulted, broken victim, beaten and bruised and maltreated almost beyond recognition—that the last sight of Jesus should be that agonized figure on the Cross. No! God will never permit that. He has stored all these things up in His heart, and the day shall come, and come soon,—for the signs of the times are heralding it,—when the world, beholding His glory and His glorious appearing, shall know that the same Jesus who was spat upon, scourged, crucified, is very God of very God.

After this shall be fulfilled God's prophecy and covenanted word: "That at the name of Jesus every knee should bow, of things in heaven, and things in earth, and things under the earth; and that every tongue should confess that Jesus Christ is Lord, to the glory of God the Father" (Phil. 2:10, 11).

Is it not another sign of the times that tracts are beginning to appear which are intended for those who will be left behind, here on earth, at the mercy of the awful activities of Satan and godless men after the Church shall have been caught up out of this world to meet the Lord in the air (1 Thess. 4:16, 17)? I have seen a four-page tract entitled "A Guide to those who are left to go through the Great Tribulation, after the Rapture of the True Church." The first page bears the statement:

> The coming of the Lord Jesus Christ for His saints, and the counsel given in this pamphlet, may not be of any interest to you now. But we earnestly counsel you to put this information some place where it will be safely kept, and where you can find it, in case you want to regard its message at a future day.

The message of the tract is "To those who are left," and it explains the rapture or catching away of the Church, which the tract says "has taken place" (this is intended to be read, of course, after the rapture), and then it explains that the "church" remaining on earth is not the true church but the apostate Church of Laodicea, spewed out of the Lord's mouth (Rev. 3:16). A frank statement is made concerning the terrible times that lie immediately ahead in the tribulation, the persecution and martyrdom that await those who will now live for Christ, but the sure salvation promised to those who will endure to the end (Matt. 24:13). This counsel is given: "Study your Bible earnestly while you have it, and memorize as much as possible before it is taken from you." There is an urgent call to accept Christ as Saviour now, if one sees this leaflet before the Church is taken away. And there is the note: "Thoughtful business men in this country are putting this information in their safe deposit boxes, together with their wills and other valuables, and if you are wise you will do the same. If you don't need it, others left behind will." [1]

Let us remember that it is possible to have a merely intel-

---

[1] This leaflet, *A Guide after the Rapture*, is printed by the Sheffield Press, 503 S. Cabrillo, San Pedro, Calif.

lectual interest and belief in the Second Coming of Christ which may be lacking in the deep love of His appearing that God's Word pleads with His children to have and to show forth. It is possible to be a fervent believer in the Lord's return, and to emphasize and drive home this truth in such a loveless and even antagonistic way that men are driven away from it instead of being won to it. And it is possible, on the other hand, to love the Lord truly without realizing the Scriptural truth and blessing of "that blessed hope."

A well known Christian leader, who for many years has rejoiced in the truth of the Lord's return, has told of a remark made by his own father many years ago. His father was a devoted and consecrated Christian, but of an earlier generation that had not been taught the truths of prophecy and the Second Coming, and he had never succeeded in grasping this truth. One day he said to his son: "I do not understand the teachings of the Bible as you see it, concerning the Second Coming of Christ. But I do want to say this: If you are right in your understanding of this matter, and if our Lord should come again today, or at any moment, I do not believe there is anyone on earth who would love to see Him more than I would." Here was a child of God who certainly must be included among those who "love His appearing." And we should be slow to criticize fellow-Christians whose hearts are right with God, and who truly love their Lord, yet who may not have come into a clear understanding of the truth of the Lord's return.

A few years ago I was with a group of Christian friends at luncheon, and after the meal I was asked, quite unexpectedly, to give a brief Scripture message. As I looked round the group and realized that everyone present held uncompromisingly to all the precious fundamentals of the faith, including the blessed hope of the imminent return of the Lord, I was led to mention a thought that had recently come to me as to a paraphrase that might be given of the last verse of the 13th chapter of the First Corinthians— that immortal description of the love that "never faileth." The verse tells us of three precious things that abide: faith, hope, love. "Faith" believes that the Bible is the whole Word of God, believes it "from cover to cover"; and that is Fundamentalism. "Hope" is the blessed hope of the Lord's return, or Premillennialism. So we may read: "And now abideth fundamentalism, premillennialism, love, these three." Then the apostle concludes with a word that we are all too prone to forget: "But the greatest of these is love." Fundamentalism and Premillennialism without love may be "as sounding brass or a tinkling cymbal."

Those who are looking most eagerly for Christ can make Him most inviting to others. A writer in the Keswick Calendar calls attention to the two "Comes" in the last chapter of the last book of the Bible, the Revelation. The next to the last verse gives us the word of the Lord Jesus Christ Himself, "Surely I come quickly." This is followed by the response of the inspired writer John, speaking for the Church, "Even so, come, Lord Jesus." A few verses earlier we read: "And the Spirit and the Bride say, Come. And let him that heareth say, Come. And let him that is athirst come. And whosoever will, let him take the water of life freely." The comment is made: "This closing passage of the Word of God presents the Church as the Bride in right relation to Christ. And when the Bride can say 'Come' to Christ, she is ready to turn to the world around and say, 'Come.'"

There are the two "Comes." We can turn from saying with longing hearts to our Lord, "Come," and say to our unsaved neighbor, "Come to Him who alone can save you. Christ is coming soon; will you not come to Him now, that when He comes again you may be ready to receive Him?"

We can say "Come" with power to the unsaved if we say "Come" with pleading to the Saviour.

CRITICISMS, QUESTIONS, AND TESTIMONIES

In the following pages are given typical criticisms of the Scriptural teaching of the Lord's Return, practical questions that have puzzled earnest Christians, and glowing testimonies from those whose lives have been transformed by "the blessed hope."

1. "Pastor Dismisses Coming of Christ"

I enclose a portion of a sermon delivered by one of our ministers. Dissect it impartially, use it as you think best, for the edification of your readers. I believe the entire article wholly unscriptural and that, when analyzed, it fails to make common sense.

The newspaper clipping giving a portion of the sermon includes the following:

Pastor Dismisses Coming of Christ

We may write the history of mankind in a series of major disappointments which are all over the face of the human story. Through the centuries men had waited for the coming of the Messiah, but he did not come and there was great disappointment. However, a carpenter who spoke wondrous words did come. Men called him Messiah and expected him to ride in on a horse and take his place as a ruler. When he did not do these things, men would not accept him. After he was taken down from the cross, men forgot him. There were rumors on Easter morning of a living Lord, for some had seen him, and of that hope the church was born.

No one could understand how the Messiah could die, be crucified. A student of history would have told them that that was just what would happen to a Messiah in any age. But the Gospel of John proves that Jesus would never come back. Washington does not come back. Lincoln and Newton do not come back. They were to settle problems of that era. So Jesus

157

will not come back. The Gospel of John tells us why—because Jesus never went away. His spirit is always here to guide men to truth.

This is no time to be looking for the second coming of Christ, nor for the destruction of the world. It is the time to write a new chapter and to write it in the spirit of Christ, who isn't coming back because he never went away.

There are strange omissions of Scripture in this sermon, and sharp contradictions of Scripture. The whole message of the New Testament and the Old is that the Messiah *did* come in Jesus Christ, fulfilling the plain prophecies of Scripture as to what the Messiah would be and would do. Those who, like this minister, were ignorant of Scripture failed to recognize Jesus as Messiah; but many men accepted Him, and many men did not. At the beginning of Christ's ministry Andrew said to Simon, "We have found the Messiah . . . And he brought him to Jesus" (John 1:41, 42). All the apostles but Judas Iscariot recognized and confessed Him as Messiah before His death, and after His death and resurrection; and so did countless other Jews and Gentiles.

Yet it is not "students of history" that are able to understand who Christ is and why He was crucified, but only those who study and believe God's Word. For there has been but one Messiah since the world began, and He was and is the only begotten Son of God.

It is, of course, ignorant denial of God's Word to say that, as Washington, Lincoln, and Newton "do not come back" because "they were to settle problems of that era, so Jesus will not come back." That likens the only Messiah, the only Son of God, the only Saviour of sinners, the only Lord of glory and King of kings, to Washington, Lincoln, and Newton—and the believer recoils from such darkened and blinded thinking.

The sermon then contradicts itself, for it says something in direct conflict with what it has just said. John's Gospel tells us, says this preacher, that Jesus will not come back "because Jesus never went away." It is to be feared that this preacher has not read John's Gospel carefully. For the last chapter, in inspired agreement with the rest of the New

Testament, shows that those believers who are living when Christ comes again will never die, and it records the mistaken report circulated among the early Christians that John was to live until the Lord's return and therefore would not die. "Then went this saying abroad among the brethren, that that disciple should not die: yet Jesus said not unto him, He shall not die; but, if I will that he tarry till I come, what is that to thee?" (John 21:23.) "Till I come," can mean nothing but the Second Coming of Christ. By no possible exegis can it refer to the coming of the Holy Spirit, as the California preacher tries to assure us, for a few weeks after the Lord spoke those words the Holy Spirit came upon the Church to abide; *and later all the apostles died.*

Moreover the New Testament, all of which was written after the death, resurrection, and ascension of Christ and the coming of the Holy Spirit, is filled with statements that Christ is coming again in personal, visible, bodily presence, just as Christ himself taught (Matt. 24:27; Luke 21:27). What, for example, are we to do with this plain statement made to the disciples as they "looked stedfastly toward heaven as he [Christ] went up" in his ascension: "this same Jesus, which is taken up from you into heaven, shall so come in like manner as ye have seen him go into heaven"? (Acts 1:11.) Would those who deny the Second Coming of Christ try to persuade us that this refers to the coming of the Holy Spirit on the day of Pentecost, or the coming of Christ into the hearts of men when they receive Him as Saviour?

Does the following statement describe the coming of the Holy Spirit "to guide men to truth"? "For the Lord himself shall descend from heaven with a shout, with the voice of the archangel, and with the trump of God: and the dead in Christ shall rise first: then we which are alive and remain shall be caught up together with them in the clouds, to meet the Lord in the air: and so shall we ever be with the Lord" (1 Thess. 4:16, 17).

If the Lord Jesus Christ "never went away," why does Paul write by inspiration, "having a desire to depart, and to be with Christ; which is far better"? (Phil. 1:23.) It is Scripturally true, of course, that Christ indwells every believer, and that He is with the Church here on earth: "I am with you alway, even unto the end of the world [age] (Matt. 28:20). But it is also true, because plainly declared in the Scriptures, that in His risen and glorified body He went away and is today in Heaven, seated at the right hand of God (Eph. 1:20; Col. 3:1; Heb. 1:3; 12:2). It is in that same glorified body that He will leave Heaven and come again to this earth as He promised.

But not to destroy this earth! The California minister, not knowing the Scriptures or "that blessed hope" of believers, makes the usual mistake of thinking that the Second Coming of Christ means "the destruction of the world." It means exactly the opposite—the redemption of this earth. "For we know that the whole creation groaneth and travaileth in pain together until now" (Rom. 8:22), waiting for the Lord's return, when he will establish His kingdom on earth and reign over this earth for a thousand years. It will be a redemption indeed for the earth; Eden conditions will be restored; wars will cease, and "the earth shall be full of the knowledge of the Lord, as the waters cover the sea" (Isa. 11:9).

If the California preacher is right when he tells us, "This is no time to be looking for the Second Coming of Christ," then we must have a new Bible and a new Christ! For the Lord Himself said, as He told His disciples about His Second Coming in His great Olivet Discourse answering their plain question, "What shall be the sign of thy coming, and of the end of the world [age]?": "And what I say unto you I say unto all, Watch" (Mark 13:37). After describing the conditions that should prevail among men and on this earth just before His Second Coming, in a detailed prophecy which is being fulfilled in the most convincing way today before our eyes, the Lord said: "And when these things begin to come to pass, then look up, and lift up your heads; for your redemption draweth nigh" (Luke 21:28).

The newspaper report of this sermon bears the headline, "Pastor Dismisses Coming of Christ." But God has not dismissed it! He has promised it, and "all the promises of God in him are yea, and in him Amen" (2 Cor. 1:20). This is the time of all times "to be looking for the Second Coming of Christ," for, whenever He may come, His coming is nearer than ever before. There are wonderful promises made "unto all them also that love his appearing" (2 Tim. 4:8). And the last promise in the Bible is from the lips of the Lord Jesus Himself, "Surely I come quickly." Although nineteen centuries have passed since our Lord spoke those words, His coming will be "quickly" in contrast with the eternity of blessing that will follow. He longs to have all men join in the last prayer of the Bible: "Even so, come, Lord Jesus."

2. Is the Second Coming of Christ "All Speculation"?

I have enjoyed reading your articles on the Lord's return.

The doctrine of the second coming came into our lives through our mutual friends, Ralph and Edith Norton, for which we are thankful.

The Scofield Reference Bible came into our house through a suggestion from these same friends, for which we are also thankful.

At one time we had a pastor who would not even talk about the second coming. Said it was "all speculation" and that "no one knows anything about it."

One recent stormy Sunday morning I was unable to attend church on account of ill health. I turned the radio on. A noted divine gave a religious talk and then answered questions. One question was "Is it true that Jesus is coming back to set up his Kingdom on earth and rule over the world?"

Answer: "Many people think so, but I do not. I do not see why he should. He came in the first place with his message of love, showing men how to live, how to meet the experiences of life, and I cannot see how it would make it more powerful or how it would help any to have him come again, and therefore I do not believe he is coming."

The astounding thing about this reply is that this minister did not refer to the Bible at all. He did not say that the Bible says something about this. He did not even say that "probably what the Bible did say was made up and written by the disciples long after Jesus departed." Nor did he say that "any prophecies in the Bible about the Lord's return have been fulfilled spiritually." He said nothing along this line.

He said that, according to his reason, his wisdom, his intellect, it would not do any good, it would not help matters, and therefore Christ was not coming.

The sad thing about this reply is that here was a nationally (perhaps internationally) famous religious leader speaking over a net work from coast to coast. Probably millions heard the question and heard the answer. Perhaps ninety-nine out of every hundred, or rather 999 out of every 1,000, would take a reply from such a source as final and conclusive and accept it as the truth without a semblance of a doubt.

We are not disturbed by the opinions of any man, no matter how high his standing. We are resting on the Word of God.

Those who, like this minister, take what they call the "Modernist" view of religion pride themselves on using their intellects and being strictly rational and logical. The strange fact about their position is that, like this minister who says the Second Coming of Christ is "all speculation" and that "no one knows anything about it," such Modernists do not realize that they are irrational and illogical to an amazing degree, and that they fail completely to put the question to an intellectual test.

This minister, for example, says he sees no reason why Christ should come again, and this is the way he proves it: Christ came in the first place with His message of love, showing men how to live; He gave His message fully, and He did His work; therefore it would not "help any to have Him come again." But how does this minister *know* that Christ came in the first place with His message of love and showed men how to live? He knows it only because he reads it in a certain book called the Bible. There, and there only, does this minister find full and authoritative historical records of Christ's first coming and of His message of love and His teaching men how to live. This same book, the Bible, which is the minister's source-book and authority for all that he knows of Christ, declares throughout its pages that Christ is coming again. The truth of the Second Coming is given more than three hundred times in the New Testament alone. Christ Himself declared it repeatedly; the divine lips that uttered His "message of love" said also, "I will come again" (John 14:3). But that, doubtless says this minister with many others who, abandoning reason, logic, and intellect, accept what they please in the Bible and reject what they please, means only that Christ comes into the hearts of all who receive Him. If that is so, then what do these words spoken by our Lord mean? "For as the lightning cometh out of the east, and shineth even unto the west; so shall also the coming of the Son of man be . . . and they shall see the Son of man coming in the clouds of heaven with power, and great glory" (Matt. 24:27-30). Is that how Christ comes into the heart of the believer?

The late greatly beloved "Valiant for Truth," Dr. J. Gresham Machen, showed with unanswerable logic and brilliant reasoning in his published writings, and in his addresses to students and mature men of trained minds, that so-called Modernism is anti-intellectualism, fundamentally lacking in the simplest elements of intellectual thought, and that it abandons any attempt to reason from accepted premises to logical conclusions. This is inevitable, for the foundation of Modernism is the denial of some part of God's Word. When men begin to call the truth a lie, they have started down the road that leads to mental atrophy, intellectual blindness, and moral death.

If the Second Coming of Christ is all speculation and no one knows anything about it, then the person of Christ, His earthly ministry, His death and resurrection, and any Gospel for lost sinners are all speculation and no one knows anything about them. If the Second Coming of Christ is speculative, so is His first coming. There is no more reason to believe that "God so loved the world, that he gave his only begotten Son, that whosoever believeth in him should not perish, but have everlasting life," than to believe that "this same Jesus, which is taken up from you into heaven, shall so come in like manner as ye have seen him go into heaven" (John 3:16; Acts 1:11). But, God be praised, *neither of these statements is speculative!* We know that both are true, "For the Son of God, Jesus Christ, who was preached among you . . . was not yea and nay, but in him was yea. For all the promises of God in him are yea, and in him Amen" (2 Cor. 1:19, 20).

3. True Scholarship and the Second Coming of Christ

Can belief in God's Word and true scholarship go together? One must confess to strange and inexcusable ignorance if he doubts this. President Eggleston, of Hampden-Sydney College, whose graduates have totaled a larger number in the biographical volume of leaders in various fields known as *Who's Who in America* than any other American college or university, wrote a notable series of articles for *The Sunday School Times* in 1936 on great scientists who were true Christians and staunch believers in the Scriptures. Such a scholar, scientist, and surgeon, honored by the learned societies of Europe and America, as Dr. Howard A. Kelly of Johns Hopkins University finds his scholarship and his implicit faith in God's Word, including belief in the personal return of the Lord, in no way incompatible. A long list of outstanding Bible scholars could be given, including such giants as the late Dr. W. H. Griffith Thomas, as an impressive roll call of those holding "that blessed hope" of the Lord's return as one of the clearly revealed and precious fundamentals of Scriptural truth.

It is a well known fact that the "discovery" of the Second Coming of Christ has revolutionized lives and made the Bible a new book to many. Letters from two aged ministers are given elsewhere in this volume (pages 16, 186), each telling how his discovery of the premillennial second coming of Christ, late in life, marked a new beginning of Christian life and Bible study; one of these ministers, now seventy-seven, lived sixty-two years without the Blessed Hope; the other, now almost ninety, lived seventy years without this knowledge. Both of them are now thanking the Lord that their eyes were opened, and rejoice to be among those who "love His appearing."

It is just as thrilling a discovery to young people as to older ones. The following letter from a Pennsylvania reader tells of a boy who was awakened and thrilled by the same discovery.

An issue of *The Sunday School Times* arrived Monday night. Tuesday morning it went out as a missionary in the pocket of a neighboring high school senior. One splendid young fellow read parts of it during a spare period. He had never before heard one word of the Second Coming or of present events in any way fulfilling Bible prophecy. He went home at noon, hunted up everything that he could find by himself (totally ignorant of how or where to look), came back bursting with questions and interest. He is the outstanding history student in this district.

It may be interesting to know that through my giving a message on the necessity of believing and looking for Christ to come—with the story of Simeon as a basis—I was invited by my pastor to cease teaching in his church. He accused me of ignorance and being a back number, said no "scholar" believed any such stuff today. I really thought his definition of scholar needed reconstruction, but, thank God, not one vestige of bitterness was aroused in my heart. Instead, a burden of prayer which had been placed on my heart for him even before I met him has been intensified. With a God-given fervor and a Spirit-filled message, what a power for Christ he might be! He is really sincere, I am sure, but totally ignorant of real truth. He simple believes what he has been taught at a theological seminary near here.

We are hearing of some of the bigger folks in church circles being put "on the spot" by Modernists. I wonder if you have any idea how universally it is happening to laymen. I know of seventeen among my own acquaintances who in the last two years have been forced out, or smothered out of any chance to teach in the churches they were attending. This high school boy of whom I speak has been treated worse in the church which holds his membership than by his professors in high school, one of whom is an atheist. He has fearlessly stood out against evolution (changed his teacher's point of view by his debate against it), against the modern ideas prevalent in problems of democracy, and has been allowed to give his original oration treating the Bible side of peace before his high school and in the district contest. He even set his high school principal to thinking and questioning him, making him miss several classes.

Maybe God is forcing us out of the house where we are not received, that our witnessing may reach farther to those who are sincerely ignorant but nevertheless hungry.

4. "This Generation Shall Not Pass, Till"

I am much interested in your articles on Christ's Second Coming, I believe it is a precious hope, but I always come against such passages as Matthew 16:27, 28 and Mark 13:30, and I am completely baffled. That generation and many more have passed and Christ has not yet come. Can you explain this?

Our Lord said to his disciples: "For the Son of man shall come in the glory of his Father with his angels; and then he shall reward every man according to his works." Then the Lord continued with the statement that has troubled this reader and other Christians: "Verily I say unto you, There be some standing here, which shall not taste of death, till they see the Son of man coming in his kingdom" (Matt. 16:28).

Yet the meaning of our Lord's words is plain from other Scriptures, and has long been recognized by students of the Word. Two passages explain what the Lord meant when He predicted—and Christ could not lie—that some of those to whom He was speaking should, before they died, "see the Son of man coming in his kingdom." The first explanatory passage immediately follows that verse; the second is in an inspired Letter written by one of the disciples to whom the Lord was speaking.

There were no chapter or verse divisions in the original manuscripts of the New Testament, these having been made later for ease in reading and reference; therefore the closing verses of Matthew 16 and the opening verses of chapter 17 make a continuous narrative, with no chapter-break or division between them. So Matthew's Gospel records, immediately after this prediction by our Lord, the fulfillment of the prediction: "And after six days Jesus taketh Peter, James, and John his brother, and bringeth them up into an high mountain apart, and was transfigured before them: and his face did shin as the sun, and his raiment was white as the light." There was Christ glorified, appearing to His disciples in a preview, as it were, of His kingdom.

The Scofield Reference Bible gives this illuminating comment, which expresses the view of sound and evangelical commentators generally:

The transfiguration scene contains, in miniature, all the elements of the future kingdom in manifestation: (1) The Lord, not in humiliation, but in glory (v. 2). (2) Moses, glorified, representative of the redeemed who have passed through death into the kingdom (Matt. 13:43; cf. Luke 9:30, 31). (3) Elijah, glorified, representative of the redeemed who have entered the kingdom by translation (1 Cor. 15:50-53; 1 Thess. 4:14-17). (4) Peter, James, and John, not glorified, representatives (for the moment) of Israel in the flesh in the future kingdom (Ezek. 37:21-27). (5) The multitude at the foot of the mountain (v. 14), representative of the nations who are to be brought into the kingdom after it is established over Israel (Isa. 11:10-12, etc.).

That this interpretation is not merely a fallible human opinion is seen from what Peter himself wrote by inspiration more than thirty years later. Peter was one of the three specially privileged disciples to witness this great sight of "the Son of man coming in his kingdom," and he has much to say in his two Epistles about the second coming of Christ. His inspired interpretation of our Lord's transfiguration on the mount is this:

For we have not followed cunningly devised fables, *when we made known unto you the power and coming of our Lord Jesus Christ, but were eyewitnesses of his majesty.* For he received from God the Father honor and glory, when there came such a voice to him from the excellent glory, This is my beloved Son, in whom I am well pleased. And this voice which came from heaven we heard, when we were with him in the holy mount.

Peter, then, knew what "the power and coming of our Lord Jesus Christ" is to be, for he was one of the three chosen "eyewitnesses of his majesty."

The passage in Mark 13:30 that has puzzled this reader is part of the great Olivet Discourse of our Lord, in which He answered His disciples' question about the end of the age and His Second Coming. He described in detail many startling events that would characterize the end of the age and herald His return, and then He said: "Verily I say unto you, that this generation shall not pass, till all these things be done."

Those who deny the inspiration of the Bible and, by their denial, fulfill prophecy by scoffing at the "blessed hope" of the Lord's return as Peter said they would (2 Pet. 3:4), even go so far as to say that Mark 13:30 shows that the Lord Jesus Christ was mistaken; that He thought something was going to happen which did not happen, inasmuch as the "generation" to whom He spoke those words did pass and the things He predicted did not occur. It is significant, in view of this popular unbelief, that the Lord said immediately after making His prediction: "Heaven and earth shall pass away: *but my words shall not pass away*" (Mark 13:31).

There are two reasonable explanations of our Lord's prediction; either one of them may be correct, or they may both be correct, as they do not conflict. One explanation is that by the word "generation" our Lord was referring to the Jews as a national entity, Israel as a people; and that He meant that God would not permit the Jews to disappear from the earth, or "pass, till all these things be done." The preservation and perpetuation of Israel as a distinct people among all the nations of the earth is a miracle of God's ordaining, for if men could have had their way the Jews would have been destroyed from the face of the earth long before now. The Scofield Reference Bible gives this interpretation in a note on the parallel passage in Matthew 24:34, calling attention to the fact that the Greek word translated "generation" is *genea,* and that the primary definition of this word is "race, kind, family, stock, breed. That the word is used in this sense here is sure because none of 'these things,' i.e., the world-wide preaching of the kingdom, the great tribulation, the return of the Lord in visible glory, and the regathering of the elect, occurred at the destruction of Jerusalem by Titus, A.D. 70. The promise is, therefore, that the generation—nation, or family of Israel—will be preserved unto 'these things'; a promise wonderfully fulfilled to this day."

Another explanation of the verse is that the Lord meant that the generation in which the predicted signs of the end of the age *begin* to occur will not pass until all the predictions are fulfilled and the Lord himself has returned. For the verse is preceded by this statement from the Lord:

Now learn a parable of the fig tree; When her branch is yet tender, and putteth forth leaves, ye know that summer is near: so ye in like manner, when ye shall see these things come to pass, know that it [the Second Coming of the Son of man] is nigh, even at the doors.

5. Does "Fig Tree" Mean the Jews?

You say, "The fig tree is one of the Bible symbols for the Jew." I see that statement made frequently, but can find no Biblical evidence for it.

In Jeremiah 24:1-8 God makes figs a symbol of Judah, or the Jews. He shows the prophet Jeremiah two baskets of figs, one basket having "very good figs," and the other basket "very evil, that cannot be eaten, they are so evil." Then God explains the meaning of these baskets of figs, saying that the good figs symbolize the Jews that God is sending into captivity "for their good," whom God will bring back again to their land; and the evil figs stand for the Jews that have turned against God.

There are New Testament passages concerning the fig tree which, while not giving as direct a statement as that in Jeremiah that the fig is a type of Israel, nevertheless leave us in no doubt that it is. The thought of fruit-bearing with relation to Israel is prominent in our Lord's teachings, and when He cursed the barren fig tree because it bore no fruit (Matt. 21:18-20) He was plainly making this incident a parable-in-fact to show the curse that was to come upon Israel because of her barren, fruitless condition.

So of the parable of the fig tree that our Lord spoke in His great Olivet Discourse of prophecy: "Now learn a parable of the fig tree; when his branch is yet tender, and putteth forth leaves, ye know that summer is nigh: so likewise ye, when ye shall see all these things, know that it is near, even at the doors" (Matt. 24:32, 33). This cannot mean anything but a reference to Israel as a nation. The *Davis Bible Dictionary*, together with other sound commentaries, says: "The barren fig tree of our Lord's parable meant the Jewish nation."

Another parable of the fig tree, plainly referring to Israel, is in Luke 13:6-9, where the owner of a vineyard, finding no fruit on a certain fig tree, orders it cut down.

Israel, the fig tree, is indeed putting forth leaves in fulfillment of prophecy, as chapters in this volume show. Zionism, or the return of the Jews to their land, and the turning of individual Jews to Christ as their Messiah and

Saviour, are signs of the budding of the fig tree for which we may well thank God and take courage.

6. Is Prophecy Being Fulfilled in Palestine Today?

A remarkable volume was published in 1935, written by George T. B. Davis, entitled *Rebuilding Palestine According to Prophecy*. Mr. Davis visited Palestine in 1931 and again in 1935, and told of the astonishing developments that had taken place there in four short years. He said:

It is a study of fascinating interest and confirms one's faith in the supernatural inspiration of the Word of God, to see how all this rebuilding and reconstruction of the land is taking place today before our eyes *exactly as foretold by the Old Testament prophets thousands of years ago*. For several years the Jews have been returning to their homeland at the rate of tens of thousands annually from many lands.[1]

But the question has been raised whether the remarkable rehabilitation of Palestine in its colonization, building achievements, and agricultural development, and the return of the Jews in the movement known as Zionism, is really a fulfillment of Bible prophecy. The Jews are returning to their land today in unbelief; the vast majority of them have not recognized the Lord Jesus Christ as Israel's divinely promised Messiah. Is this independent of prophecy, or is it related to God's prophetic Word? Is God back of present Zionism, or is Satan? Does the Bible predict the Jews' return in unbelief, or only in belief?

These questions have been raised, and they are of importance to our understanding of Bible prophecy and the Jew of today. A number of well known Bible teachers were asked by *The Sunday School Times* for their views on these questions, and their replies are of exceptional value.

The Rev. H. A. Ironside, Litt.D.

I do not believe that the present return of the Jews to Palestine is the work of Satan. I see in it the overruling

[1] The book with many full-page photographs, *Rebuilding Palestine According to Prophecy*, is published by The Million Testaments Campaigns, 1505 Race Street, Philadelphia, at 25 cents, paper; 50 cents, cloth; postpaid.

hand of God, preparing the people and the land for the events of the last days. I take my position absolutely with you and with Mr. Davis in regard to the statement that the Jews are going back to the land of their fathers in unbelief, precisely as God foretold.

Many passages of prophecy make it perfectly plain that in the last days, after the rapture of the Church, the people of Israel in large numbers will already be in the land, but the very fact that they will be left behind when the Church is caught up makes it plain that they are there in unbelief. The Spirit of God, however, will begin a mighty work immediately following the translation of the Church. "The wise shall understand." "And they that understand among the people shall instruct many" (Dan. 12:10; 11:33). A witnessing remnant will be separated from the mass of the people, who will be used of God to lead many of their breathren to repentance. It will be an Elijah-like ministry such as that of John the Baptist, really carrying on John the Baptist's testimony, preparing the people for the return of the Lord and the setting up of the Kingdom. To say that Satan is the agent in bringing these Jews back to the land is, to my mind, a complete ignoring of the fact that God is still on the throne and is the moral governor of the universe, "who worketh all things after the counsel of his own will" (Eph. 1:11).

William L. Pettingill, D.D.

The great basic passage showing that the Jews must return in unbelief to their land is Daniel 9, where the Beast makes "the covenant with many" in Israel (v. 27), which would be impossible if the Jews were not still in unbelief.

Arthur J. Brown, M.D., F.R.C.S.

God is bringing to pass His will, and in so doing is using many instruments—Hitler, Satan, and many others.

The divine condition of inheriting the land in the sense of enjoying the fullest possible blessing is, of course, contingent on obedience, but certainly that does not apply to the *return* to the land; and before the Jews can be blessed *in* the land it is obvious that they must be brought back *to* it. There is no statement in the Bible that they will return in obedience—rather just the opposite.

The German Jews are being driven, *much against their will*, to their homeland. Is it not possible and even probable that God might use the Devil if that is necessary to bring to fruition His plans and purpose?

The Jews are driven or brought back to their land, many means being used, the chief being persecution. They will undergo the fierce fires of tribulation there and in other lands where they are still living. *Then* they will be brought to a realization that obedience is necessary, and the greater blessings will come, fulfilling every detail of the glorious prophecies relating to them.

God said: "I will cause them to return." "The wastes shall be builded." The people *are* returning, the wastes *are* being built. This is obviously fulfilled prophecy.

The Rev. Graham Gilmer

The Scriptures clearly predict what we see beginning to take place in the return of the Jews to the Promised Land. There are between sixteen and eighteen million Jews in the world today. It is not predicted that all of these will return to Palestine before the coming of Christ to establish his Kingdom. In fact, the land could not at present sustain them. Christ tells us what He will do in regard to this. "He shall send forth his angels with a great sound of a trumpet, and they shall gather together his elect from the four winds, from one end of heaven to the other" (Matt. 24:31). "His elect" refers to his elect nation Israel.

"Shall a land be born in one day? shall a nation be brought forth at once? for as soon as Zion travailed she brought forth her children" (Isa. 66:8). This national conversion will take place in every part of the world at the same time. We are taught something of this in the thirtieth chapter of Deuteronomy. They will call God's truth to mind among all the nations whither Jehovah has driven them, "and shalt return unto Jehovah thy God, and shalt obey his voice" (Deut. 30:1, 2).

Again, something of this is revealed in the twentieth chapter of Ezekiel. When God gets ready to bring them back into their own land He will bring them into "the wilderness of the peoples" (Ezek. 20:35), and there will He enter into judgment with them face to face. His wrath will undoubtedly be poured out upon them all over the world. The rebels will be purged out as they pass under the rod. They will then be gathered back and established in their own land (Ezek. 20:35-38).

Before this world-wide judgment is poured out a part of the nation will be gathered back to the land in unbelief. There are several passages that teach this. In the thirty-sixth chapter of Ezekiel we hear God speaking to the mountains and to the hills, to the water courses and the valleys, to the desolate wastes and to the cities that are forsaken, telling them that He is going to restore them to their former prosperity. Then He speaks to the House of Israel and tells them that He is not doing this because of their goodness, but for His holy name (36:22). He promises to take them from among the nations and gather them out of the countries and bring them into their own land. "And I will sprinkle clean water upon you, and ye shall be clean: from all your filthiness, and from all your idols, will I cleanse you. A new heart also will I give you" (36:25,26). This cleansing is not accomplished for the remnant of the nation until after they go back into the land. They go back in unbelief.

The conversion of these people is discussed for us in Zechariah 12, 13, as taking place in the land. "The spirit of grace and supplication" is poured out upon "the inhabitants of Jerusalem." "In that day there shall be a fountain opened to the house of David and to the inhabitants of Jerusalem, for sin and for uncleanness." As we see from Zechariah 14:4, this will be just before the return of Christ. As will be the case of judgment falling upon those scattered among the nations, so here many will be cut off, for they remain in rebellion (14:2). Some of the people will have returned in unbelief.

There is an interesting passage in Zephaniah in regard to this. In the first chapter the prophet describes the coming day of Jehovah's wrath. Then notice what he says (1:1, 2, R. V.): "Gather yourselves together, yea, gather together, O nation that hath no shame [longing]; before the decree bring forth, before the day pass as the chaff, before the fierce anger of Jehovah come upon you." The nation will be gathering back in the land without the true longing that real repentance brings.

We find from Daniel 9:27 that "many" are in the land, having resumed the temple sacrifices, at the time of the end of this dispensation. These people are there in unbelief, even though they are going through their former ritual, for they make a firm covenant with the coming Roman Emperor, the man of sin.

Thus we find that God's Word teaches that just before the return of Christ wrath will be poured out upon Israel scattered among the nations, but we also find that before that time "many" will have returned to the land in unbelief.

George T. B. Davis

Here are some passages that seem to me to predict clearly the return of the Jews to Palestine in unbelief.

Zechariah 12:10. This seems to teach quite clearly that the Jews as a nation will remain in unbelief until they look upon the Lord when he returns.

Zechariah 13:1 states that "in that day"—the day of the Lord's return—"there shall be a fountain opened to the house of David and to the inhabitants of Jerusalem for sin and for uncleanness."

Zephaniah 3:8, 9, indicate that it is when the nations are gathered together against the Jews that the Lord will "turn to the people a pure language, that they may all call upon the name of the Lord, to serve him with one consent."

1 Corinthians 15:8 declares that Paul's vision of the glorified Christ and his consequent conversion was like that of "one born out of due time." May not this imply that Paul's conversion, through seeing the glorified Christ, is a type of the conversion of the Jews as a nation who will look upon Christ and believe in Him when he returns in glory? This will fulfill Isaiah 66:8, when a nation will be born "at once."

Romans 11:25, 26. Verse 25 states clearly that the present blindness of the Jews as a nation will continue "until the fulness of the Gentiles be come in." Verse 26 declares that it is when the Deliverer comes out of Zion that Israel shall be saved and Jacob shall be delivered from ungodliness.

These Scriptures show that the Jews as a nation will not be saved until the return of the Lord. Hence the present return of the Jews to Palestine must necessarily be in unbelief, since we are still waiting for the Lord to appear in glory, after He comes for his Church—His Bride.

The Rev. D. M. Panton

(In *The Dawn* of February 15, 1937, edited by Mr. Panton, is an illuminating article on "Zionism" in which the following statements are made):

The most vivid proof that a great and godless Zionism is assumed in Scripture without being directly foretold is the explicit statement of a rebuilt Temple. The Man of Sin, Paul says (2 Thess. 2:4), "sitteth in THE TEMPLE OF GOD, setting himself forth as God"; and the signal given by our Lord for the Jewish flight is the Antichrist's image "standing *in the holy place*" (Matt. 24:15). . . .

Thus Zionism is setting the stage for the last drama. The Lord's descent into the Parousia finds an Israel in the Holy Land closely akin to the Israel He found when He descended to Bethlehem; and an identical massacre succeeds. All nations swarm down, in anti-Semitic fury, on Jerusalem (Zech. 14:2); and "it shall come to pass that in all the land, saith the Lord, two parts therein shall be cut off and die" (Zech. 13:8),[1] "and half of the city shall go forth into captivity" (Zech. 14:2). In the seven years' struggle with the Roman Power, which followed the Crucifixion, one million and a half Jews perished, 580,000 at the fall of Bithar alone: so shall it be again. But exactly as "a remnant according to the election of grace" (Rom. 11:5) has escaped into the Church, so again—apart from the 144,000 who have already escaped into the wilderness (Matt. 24:16; Rev. 7:4)—a remnant is purged through fire. "And I will bring the third part through the fire, and will refine them

---

[1] Exactly this is what an Arab paper in Jerusalem has already voiced. "In a crescendo of hate," says the Special Correspondent of the *Daily Telegraph* (Jan. 7, 1937) in Palestine, "the country, if necessary, shall be made one huge grave, and the dead will arise from the Moslem cemeteries to help in the process."

as silver is refined, and will try them as gold is tried: they shall call on my name, and I will hear them: I will say, it is my people; and they shall say, The Lord is my God" (Zech. 13:9).

So Armageddon follows, and the descent on Olivet. *"Then* shall the Lord go forth, and fight against those nations; and his feet shall stand in that day upon the Mount of Olives" (Zech. 14:3). The divine Zionism follows, a vast and supernatural exodus out of all lands of the nation no longer Lo Ammi, "not my people," but once more the People of God, for they have seen the King.

Note by the Author

It must be recognized, of course, that the complete fulfillment of some of the Old Testament prophecies relating to Israel's final restoration to her land must await her recognition of Christ as her Messiah and her turning to Him in repentance, confession, and faith. But the prophecy of the dry bones brought to life, as given in Ezekiel 37, would seem to indicate just what is occurring before our eyes today in Zionism and in Palestine. Israel complains, "Our bones are dried, and our hope is lost." The prophet declares: "Thus saith the Lord God; behold, O my people, I will open your graves, and cause you to come up out of your graves, and bring you into the land of Israel." This, apparently, is what God is doing today with Israel. It is only *after* this prediction that the prophet goes on to predict something that will occur later: "And shall put my spirit in you, and ye shall live, and I shall place you in your own land." In other words, God brings Israel into the land while she is still in unbelief; later, at the coming of the Lord, when Israel turns to Christ as her Messiah, God's Spirit enters into His people, and then there is a national restoration to the land beyond anything that can occur before that time. For there will be a tremendously greater return to the land by the Jews, from all parts of the world, after they have turned to Christ as their Messiah.

The Scofield Reference Bible takes this view in the note on Ezekiel 37: "The 'graves' are the nations where they dwell. The order of procedure is: (1) the bringing of the people out (v. 12); (2) the bringing of them in (v. 12); (3) their conversion (v. 13); (4) the filling with the Spirit (v. 14)."

7. WILL THE ROMAN EMPIRE BE RESTORED?

A dear friend of mine, a devout Christian, seems never to have heard that the Roman Empire will be revived just before the Second Coming of Christ. I don't feel I could do the subject justice; could you discuss it?

In 1932 the late Ralph C. Norton, who with Mrs. Norton founded and directed the Belgian Gospel Mission, was face to face with Mussolini, Premier and Dictator of Italy. He had granted a private, personal interview in the great chamber where he receives the favored few in his palace at Rome, the Palazzo di Venezia. They were alone with Il Duce, with free and unhindered opportunity for personal conversation.

"In numerous things I have read about you," Mr. Norton said to Premier Mussolini, "you give the impression that you are seeking to reconstitute the Roman Empire."

"The Roman Empire," he replied, "is dead. It is impossible to revive a dead thing."

"But, Your Excellency, do you know that the Roman Empire is *going* to be restored? Signor Mussolini, permit me to say that you are a man of destiny, you are a man chosen of God, because 'the powers that be are ordained of God'; but therein lies a great responsibility."

He looked at me with open eyes, but when I went on to say that the Bible says the Roman Empire is to be restored, his eyes opened wider, they gleamed, as he threw himself back in his chair and exclaimed, "WHERE?"

"In the books of Daniel and the Revelation," I continued. "It is not just simple people who believe this. You are, no doubt, well acquainted with Scotland Yard, that greatest detective system in the world. The head of Scotland Yard was the late Sir Robert Anderson, the greatest criminologist of his day in England, and he wrote some remarkable books on this subject. They are in English,— would you like to have them?"

"Yes," replied the Premier, "I should like to have them."

Mr. Norton sent Sir Robert Anderson's books and other important books on Bible prophecy and the Roman Empire to Mussolini, and the Premier must have read them with more than passing interest. Mr. Norton's article, from which the foregoing is quoted, was published in *The Sunday School Times* of April 22, 1933.

In the second chapter of Daniel we are told of a dream of Nebuchadnezzar, King of Babylon, which none of his wise men could interpret but the meaning of which was divinely revealed to Daniel. The king had seen in his dream a great image, and

This image's head was of fine gold, his breast and his arms of silver, his belly and his thighs of brass, his legs of iron, his feet part of iron and part of clay. Thou sawest till that a stone was cut out without hands, which smote the image upon his feet that were of iron and clay, and brake them to pieces. Then was the iron, the clay, the brass, the silver, and the gold, broken to pieces together, and became like the chaff of the summer threshingfloors; and the wind carried them away, that no place was found for them: and the stone that smote the image became a great mountain, and filled the whole earth (Dan. 2: 32-35).

We are given the interpretation. The great image represented four great world-kingdoms or empires, the first being Babylon under Nebuchadnezzar (Dan. 2:38). A later vision of Daniel names the second empire as Media-Persia, and the third as Greece (Dan. 8:20, 21). Concerning the fourth Sir Robert Anderson says, in his book *The Coming Prince* (out of print): "The fourth empire, therefore, must of necessity be Rome." The four world-empires are unmistakable in the light of history. We know that the "stone cut out without hands" is a symbol for Christ; other Scriptures use the same figure, such as: "This is the stone which was set at nought of you builders, which is become the head of the corner" (Acts 4:11; 1 Pet. 2:8; and other passages). The Gentile empire controlling the world at the time of the Second Coming of Christ, which will be destroyed by His coming, as seen in Nebuchadnezzar's prophetic dream, was the empire of iron and clay, the fourth empire. The fourth and last of the great world-empires in Bible times was the Roman Empire, and the prophetic

Scriptures, both in Daniel as quoted, and other Scriptures, point plainly to the revival or resurrection of the Roman Empire as the dominating government of the world when Christ shall come again.

The late Dr. I. M. Haldeman, that great Baptist preacher and student of Bible prophecy for many years in New York City, in a sermon on "The Falling Stone, or the Overthrow of the Last Kaiser," says:

To find the fourth kingdom or empire as thus doubly symbolized . . . turn to the New Testament. There we learn our Lord Jesus was born, not only under the shining stars and the angel song, but under and during the reign of Augustus Cæsar, Emperor of Rome; and that he was put to death under Tiberius Cæsar of Rome; that Rome was the great world power, the power that succeeded Greece. The characteristic element of the fourth part of the statue [in Nebuchadnezzar's dream] is *iron*. In the fourth beast the teeth are *iron* teeth. As school boys and school girls we read of "the *iron* legions of Rome."

And then, looking forward to the final World-Emperor, Cæsar, Kaiser, or Beast, foretold in Daniel and Revelation, Dr. Haldeman says:

On account of the troubled and reactionary times the ten kings will invite him to become dictator, world ruler. He will accept. He will take the title of the Prince of Rome (Daniel says he will be the prince of the people who destroyed Jerusalem. The people who destroyed Jerusalem were Romans; therefore he will be prince of the Romans, Prince of Rome). Thus will Rome be revived under its tenfold form. Elected as the head of the ten kings, he will be a king of kings, and lord of lords.

The passage referred to by Dr. Haldeman is Daniel 9:25-27.

That Mussolini has the most ambitious and far-reaching plans and purposes for the restoration of the Roman Empire is commonplace knowledge today; in the five years since Mr. Norton had his momentous interview with the Dictator, world-shaking events testifying to this have occurred.

Commenting on the Five-Year Plan that Mussolini launched at that time, Mr. Norton quoted the English *Christian Herald:*

So, for the third time in twenty-seven centuries of grandeur and decay, blood and fire, earthquake and sacking, a new city is to arise on the Seven Hills. Built by Romulus and Remus "in the year that King Uzziah died" (753 or so B. C.; Isa. 6), and rebuilt by Julius Cæsar, it is to become, under Il Duce, capable of housing a million more people than it now contains.

Underground railways are to pierce the ancient soil, powdered with the bones of Christian martyrs. Underground roads are to cleave through the hills on which the pagan watch fires burned. Motor speedways will slash the city—from east to west, north to south. "Port Mussolini," a vast harbor, will be built near the city and be linked to the sea by a fifteen mile canal, making inland Rome a great port. Two new main railway stations are to arise—the old one will be razed to the ground. A belt of parks will surround Rome. Ancient monuments, palaces, and temples are sacred; those that are cluttered up with hovels and surrounded by mean streets will be laid bare for men to see.

And much of this "resurrection of Rome" is now an accomplished fact! What will the end be? Daniel in Babylon, and John on the Island of Patmos, have answered the question, in God's infallible prophecies. The resurrected Roman Empire will be, as the Scofield Reference Bible comments on Revelation 13:1, "the last form of Gentile world-power, a confederated ten-kingdom empire covering the sphere of authority of ancient Rome." But even that mighty coming empire, supernaturally directed and empowered by Satan, will be impotent before the coming of the Son of God, the only true King of kings and Lord of lords. Then shall be fulfilled the great prophecy in Revelation 11:15, when "there were great voices in heaven, saying, The kingdoms of this world are become the kingdoms of our Lord, and of his Christ; and he shall reign for ever and ever."

8. THE RAPTURE AND THE REIGN

You quote 1 Thessalonians 4:13-18, which tells us that "the Lord himself shall descend from heaven with a shout, . . . and with the trump of God." Should we understand that that event will be the beginning of the personal reign of Christ, the beginning of the millennial period? I have read somewhere that

His coming, as described in the passage above referred to, will not be the beginning of Christ's reign, but for the purpose of taking His church out of the world. I will value any light you may give.

Such expressions as the Second Coming of Christ, the Lord's Return, and the like, are used in a general sense for Christ's leaving Heaven in order to bring to an end this present age of grace and establish his Kingdom, meaning his personal reign, on this earth. But most students of Bible prophecy who hold, as does the writer, that Christ's Second Coming is to be premillennial—that is, before the millennium and in order to establish the millennium, or the thousand-year period of his personal reign on this earth— recognize that there are two distinct stages of our Lord's return. These two stages are properly known as the Rapture and the Revelation, or the Reign. The word "rapture" means catching away, and is used to designate the experience that the Church of Christ will have at His coming, as described in the passage mentioned, 1 Thessalonians 4:13-18. This passage reads in part as follows:

For this we say unto you by the word of the Lord, that we which are alive and remain unto the coming of the Lord shall not prevent (precede) them which are asleep. For the Lord himself shall descend from heaven with a shout, with the voice of the archangel, and with the trump of God: and the dead in Christ shall rise first: then we which are alive and remain shall be caught up together with them in the clouds, to meet the Lord in the air: and so shall we ever be with the Lord.

Paul gives the same inspired prophecy in 1 Corinthians 15:51-54, where we read that "we shall not all sleep [die], but we shall all be changed, in a moment, in the twinkling of an eye, at the last trump. . . . For this corruptible must put on incorruption, and this mortal must put on immortality."

The blessed dead shall be raised at this time, and the bodies of living believers shall be changed, all being caught up "to meet the Lord in the air." When the Church has thus been taken out of the world, there will be a period of time in which the Satan-empowered Beast, or World Emperor, will be in power, and the Antichrist, with Satan directing things in supernatural power and fury, while the terrible events predicted by Daniel and other prophets, and in Revelation, will occur. The vast majority of men will worship the Beast, or World Emperor, and his image, power being "given unto him to continue forty and two months" (Rev. 13:5). The dread judgments of the Great Tribulation occur during this time, and then the age is ended by the Lord's personal, visible, bodily return to join battle with the Beast and his armies and Satan, at Armageddon, as described in Revelation 19:11-21. This is the revelation of Christ in distinction from the rapture of the Church, and His personal reign over Israel and the world follows.

A useful book that takes up these details of Bible prophecy and the Lord's return is entitled *God's Prophecies for Plain People,* a series of articles written for *The Sunday School Times* by Dr. William L. Pettingill. (The book is published by Just a Word, Inc., 1528 West Seventh St., Wilmington, Del.; $1, cloth; 50 cents, paper.)

9. AMILLENNIALISM AND THE RAPTURE

It would appear that the long-time issue between "Post" and "Pre" has demised but that a (to me) new thing, amillennialism, is rapidly coming into vogue. The point of interest to me, and the reason for this inquiry, is this: in the case of those who adopt amillennialism, what becomes of the rapture and the Second Coming? Can you refer me to some authoritative, lucid, and preferably succinct pronouncement by the new school?

The first letter in the word amillennial is the Greek *alpha,* here being the "alpha privative," meaning "without," and it is equivalent to the Latin non. Amillennial means non-millennial, or without a millennium. An apparently authoritative statement answering the question "What is Amillennialism?" was published in *The Presbyterian Guardian* (1526 Pine Street, Philadelphia) of March 27, 1937, by John Murray of the faculty of Westminster Theological Seminary. Mr. Murray's article contains these statements:

The amillennial view, as the name suggests, simply means that the amillenarian does not believe that he can find warrant in Scripture for a millennium either before or after the advent of the Lord. . . . The amillenarian *denies* a millennium after the second advent. In this denial he holds common ground with the postmillenarian. The amillenarian, in common with the postmillenarian, teaches that when Christ comes again His coming will signalize the end of the world. . . .

Why does the amillenarian deny a millennium after the Lord's return? To give all the reasons would require a book. But in brief his reason is very simple. It is just that he does not believe that the teaching of the New Testament allows such a belief. . . . In other words, he believes that the final judgement and the end of the world so coincide with the coming of the Lord that there is no room left for a millennium after the Lord's return.

Mr. Murray's article shows that amillennialism believes in the Second Coming of Christ but—strangely and unscripturally, as the writer and many evangelical believers understand God's Word—denies any millennium on earth. Mr. Murray's article said nothing about the rapture of the Church, and the writer asked him for a brief statement answering the inquirer's question and setting forth the amillennialists' understanding of the meaning of 1 Thessalonians 4:17 in relation to living believers at the time of the Second Coming of Christ—that is, as to rapture of the Church. Mr. Murray responds by sending the following statement:

The English word "rapture" is derived from a Latin word which means to seize or snatch. The Greek word corresponding to the Latin word is "harpazo" and means to "snatch away." It is this word that is used in 1 Thessalonians 4:17. Then we who are alive who remain shall be caught up together with them in clouds to meet the Lord in the air. Only in this passage does the Greek word that corresponds to our English word "rapture" occur with reference to this event.

The believers at Thessalonica were grieving over those who had departed. The occasion of their grief was apparently the thought that their dead would by reason of their departure be excluded from the joy of the coming of the Lord, or at least from some peculiar advantage that the living would experience on that event. Paul is here writing to correct that misapprehension. He tells them that the living will not have any advantage or precedence over the departed. The dead in Christ

God will lead with Christ and they will rise first. Then the living together with the resurrected dead (i. e., dead believers) will be snatched up to meet the Lord in the air. That and no more is what the "rapture" spoken of in 1 Thessalonians 4:17 teaches.

In a similar passage in 1 Corinthians 15:50-53 we are given additional information by the same Apostle that not only will the dead or those who have fallen asleep undergo the resurrection change, but the living—though not resurrected because they did not die—will also undergo a change. "We shall not all sleep, but we shall all be changed" (v. 51). And we are also told that this resurrection-change of the believing dead and change of the believing living will be "in a moment, in the twinkling of an eye, at the last trump" (v. 52). "And so shall we ever be with the Lord" (1 Thess. 4:17).

This is what amillennialists and postmillennialists believe with respect to the so-called "rapture." Their notion of the rapture is derived from the plain teaching of the passages concerned. They believe the rapture is coincident with the public, visible, personal advent of the Lord *(parousia)* and they are aware that much else occurs with respect to the righteous as accompaniment or consequence of the Lord's appearing. But they confine the idea of the rapture to *the snatching up of all believers in clouds to meet the Lord in the air.*

This statement of the amillennialist's understanding of the rapture is in agreement with the understanding of premillennialists except for the fact that most of the latter believe that the coming of the Lord for the Church, in the rapture, is invisible to the unsaved world, and that the revelation of the Lord to the whole world comes later. Most premillennialists thus believe that the rapture and the revelation are two different stages of the Lord's return, and, as was brought out in an earlier chapter in this book, that "When the Church has thus been taken out of the world, there will be a period of time in which the Satan-empowered Beast, or World Emperor, will be in power, and the Antichrist, with Satan directing things in supernatural power and fury, while the terrible events predicted by Daniel and other prophets, and in Revelation, will occur. . . . This is the revelation of Christ in distinction from the rapture of the Church, and his personal reign over Israel and the world follows."

10. WILL THE BODIES OF ALL BE RAISED FROM THE DEAD?

Are the bodies of the unsaved resurrected? Recently a Bible teacher of some note said: "The unsaved do not get back their bodies; but their bodies are cast out and are burned, and become ashes trodden under foot."

While the Lord Jesus was speaking to the Jews in Jerusalem, after He had healed a man at the pool of Bethesda, He said to them:

Marvel not at this: for the hour is coming, in the which all that are in the graves shall hear his voice, and shall come forth; they that have done good, unto the resurrection of life; and they that have done evil, unto the resurrection of damnation (John 5: 28, 29).

Both the wicked and the righteous are conscious immediately after death and before any resurrection has taken place, as is plainly shown in such a passage as Luke 16:19-31. Here the rich man in Hades saw Abraham and Lazarus afar off, across a great gulf, and carried on a conversation with Abraham. The resurrection "unto damnation," or "condemnation" as the margin gives it, must therefore mean the resurrection of the body, and there are other passages that teach the same truth.

The apostle John in the Revelation writes of the last judgment:

And I saw a great white throne, and him that sat on it, from whose face the earth and the heaven fled away; and there was no place for them. And I saw the dead, small and great, stand before God; and the books were opened: and another book was opened, which is the book of life: and the dead were judged out of those things which were written in the books, according to their works. And the sea gave up the dead which were in it; and death and hell delivered up the dead which were in them: and they were judged every man according to their works (Rev. 20:11-13).

The fact that those who were dead will stand before God at this judgment, death having delivered them up, shows that they will again have their bodies. The saved will not stand before the Great White Throne to be judged, for we have the glorious promise: "Verily, verily, I say unto you, He that heareth my word, and believeth on him that sent me, hath everlasting life, and shall not come into condemnation; but is passed from death unto life" (John 5:24); and we know also that when the Lord Jesus comes again He will "descend from heaven with a shout, with the voice of the archangel, and with the trump of God, and the dead in Christ shall rise first: then we which are alive and remain shall be caught up together with them in the clouds, to meet the Lord in the air: and so shall we ever be with the Lord" (1 Thess. 4:16, 17).

It is the great and blessed privilege of all who will in this age of grace to have part in the first resurrection, which is the resurrection of the saved. "Blessed and holy is he that hath part in the first resurrection: on such the second death hath no power, but they shall be priests of God and of Christ, and shall reign with him a thousand years" (Rev. 20:6). We may have this through faith in the Lord Jesus Christ. "Jesus said unto her, I am the resurrection, and the life: he that believeth in me, though he were dead, yet shall he live: And whosoever liveth and believeth in me shall never die. Believest thou this?" (John 11:25, 26). "For our conversation is in heaven; from whence also we look for the Saviour, the Lord Jesus Christ: who shall change our vile body, that it may be fashioned like unto his glorious body, according to the working whereby he is able even to subdue all things unto himself" (Phil. 3:20, 21).

11. A CONVERTED POSTMILLENNIALIST

A minister in Massachusetts writes:

"I am now within four months of being ninety years old, and, until twenty years ago, I was a most ardent advocate of the postmillennial theory. I had a friend with whom I had frequent debates in regard to the two great views concerning the time of the Second Coming of Christ, the premillennial and the postmillennial. These were quite heated debates,—heated so far as I was concerned,—while my friend, a lovely Christian, spoke always in a calm and concilliatory tone. Those debates took place about thirty-five years ago. Finding that she could make no impression upon me, she, to my surprise and chagrin, ceased speaking on the subject and made no reply to anything I said. In all probability she was praying for me ever after.

"But she did give me a book which she asked me to read. It was *Ecce Venit,* by the saintly Dr. A. J. Gordon. I read it at once, but with a pencil in my hand, and when I had read a page I wrote in the margin what I believed to be a complete refutation of his arguments. Then I read another page and wrote in the margin, and so on. Then I placed the book in the midst of other books in my library, and there it remained for somewhere between fifteen and twenty years, untouched.

"Then, in the afternoon of a Lord's Day as I saw that I had an hour or two to spare, I thought I would spend the time reading. I went to the book shelves and glanced along the titles, not knowing what to take. Finally my eye lighted on Dr. Gordon's book, and I was strongly impelled to take it down and glance at it again. It did not occur to me then that I was being led by the Holy Spirit, but now I know that I was, and I can never be thankful enough.

"I read a page and said to myself, 'There's nothing wrong with that. That is all right.' And I got hold of a rubber eraser and slowly and carefully erased what I had written almost twenty years before. Then I read another page, and with the same result.

"And I continued until every one of my senseless criticisms had been erased; and from that day to this I have been a most earnest student and advocate of the blessed premillennial view, and it has been the joy of my life during all these years since.

"I might say that I had once heard a lecture by Dr. Torrey on the subject in question, but that, owing to my hardness of heart and blind prejudice, it had no influence upon me. But since my eyes were opened I have found great pleasure and benefit in reading the splendid treatise on the subject by W. E. Blackstone.

"I have been engaged in the active ministry fifty years, continuing until eleven years ago, when I retired and have been living with my oldest son, who himself is engaged in the Gospel ministry and who is a faithful preacher of the whole Gospel including the imminence of the Second Coming.   During those last years of my ministry I made a business of preaching the 'Blessed Hope' in the pulpit and in the prayer meetings and in private.

"The Bible has become a new Book to me.   Passages in the Old Testament which I had always supposed referred to the Christian Church I now understand to refer to the Hebrew race; and I now see that the thought of the coming Advent runs all through the New Testament, and I am watching and longing for the speedy return of the King in His glory, that I may see His beautiful face, and hear His loving voice, and feel the pressure of His blessed hand, and may kiss those precious pierced hands and feet.   And I am praying continually that he may come speedily and say to the great enemy, 'Thus far and no farther,' and set everything right and put an end to all war and strife and misunderstandings and self-seeking, and also to all the terrible apostasy of this the 'Laodicean' age.   'Behold, I come quickly.   Even so, come, Lord Jesus.' "

12. A Missionary Who "Discovered" the Lord's Return

It used to be said, by those who were not familiar with the Scriptures or the facts of Christian service, that belief in the Second Coming of Christ "cuts the nerve of foreign missions."   The wholly theoretical, fanciful, and ignorant idea was that the people who really believe that Christ may come again at any moment are paralyzed by that belief into passivity and uselessness!   "If the Lord may come again at any moment, why should we do anything?" was the supposed attitude of those who "love his appearing."   Or again, "If the Church can never save the world, but only the Lord's return will establish righteousness, then there is no use in any Christian service before he comes."   This was the strange theory of those who were blind both to the message of the Scriptures and to the facts of missionary activity energized by "that blessed hope" of Christ's coming.   For the greatest, most consecrated, most evangelistic and indefatigable missionaries have been, like the greatest missionary of all, the apostle Paul, set on fire by the realization of the imminence of the Lord's return and its tremendous challenge and incitement to "occupy till I come" (Luke 19:13).

A striking testimony to the dynamic power of the truth of the Lord's return came in a letter from a missionary who was in America on furlough when *The Sunday School Times* was publishing a symposium of letters from leading Bible teachers and others on "How I Came to Believe in Our Lord's Return." [1] This missionary has now returned to his field in China, to labor on in his glad witness to "that blessed hope" and in his work of making souls in that vast land ready to welcome the Lord when he comes. His letter, in part, follows:

May I add my testimony to those who are giving through the pages of the *Times* "How We Came to Believe in the Lord's Return"? The discovery of the fact of our Lord's return (still future), and its application to my life, have produced such a revolutionary effect on my spiritual thinking and work that I wish humbly to tell it to the readers of your paper for its possible inspirational value.

I have been a foreign missionary under the Presbyterian Board of the U. S. A. for thirty-eight years. When I graduated from the theological seminary and went to the foreign field I was not a thorough student of the Bible. I heard the call of God to go to the foreign field. My conversion and decision to study for the Christian ministry were almost simultaneous. And I had decided for the ministry as my life work but a short time before I made the momentous decision to dedicate my life to foreign missions. This decision was based upon the simple fact of contrast in numbers of workers. There were plenty of ministers in the homeland. What reason could I give for not spending my life where most needed? I could give none, so I went to the foreign field.

For about twenty years I worked faithfully without emphasis on, or even thinking seriously of, the return of the Lord

[1] Now published in a pamphlet, "How I Came to Believe in Our Lord's Return, and Why I believe the Lord's Return Is Near," by The Bible Institute Colportage Association, 843-845 North Wells Street, Chicago, 5 cents each; 40 cents a dozen; $2.75 a hundred.

Jesus Christ. Then I passed through a crisis in my life and ministry. I became discouraged on account of paucity of results. This was true not only of the work in my immediate field, but throughout the foreign mission fields in general. It was so hard to get people to be good! It was so hard to maintain my own high standard! The world did not seem to be getting any better, except in spots—small spots at that. Nearly a century of foreign missions made an infinitesimally small impression. Persons were born faster than converts were made to Christianity. When Dr. Bradt and Dr. King came to Siam on their foreign mission tour, Dr. King's impression was that, so far as numbers are a criterion, the task is impossible. When home on furloughs I realized that our own beloved country is not really Christian —only nominally so; and, moreover, that there is no prospect of the country ever becoming wholly Christian through the efforts of Christian people, either in numbers or in spiritual quality.

I returned to the foreign field discouraged. Then one day I got hold of a Scofield Reference Bible. I read it with avidity. Dispensational truth was for the first time set out before me. The "blessed hope" of the return of our Lord became a reality. I realized that He is visiting the Gentiles, through His appointed commissioners, "to take out of them a people for his name," after which He will return again (Acts 15:13-18).

The Bible became a new Book to me. The glory of the Lord shone through its pages in a new and living way. The awful condition of the world became explicable. I was fired with a new zeal to preach, teach, and save souls. I caught a new vision of Christ in His relation to prophecy, in His atoning work, in His resurrection and intercessory work during this age of grace, in His plan for the "called-out ones" to take the Gospel unto the ends of the earth and to "every creature." My heart was set on fire to preach the Gospel, to witness to every creature. It was like being born again. My conversion was quite clear and vivid. I remember the room where it took place and the words of the preacher that brought me to Christ. That was a new birth unto salvation. A quarter of a century later I experienced another birth—a birth unto dispensational truth, including the return of our Lord.

With this vision my wife and I went, with other associates, into a pioneer field of Yunnan, China, where the Gospel was unknown and where thousands have now been led to the Saviour. The command of our Lord, the vision of the coming King, have led us into mud hovels where livestock and human beings exist under the same roof in dirt and grime and filth and smoke, and through perils of robbers in order to seek the lost and to help the Lord Jesus "take out a people for his name."   And when this is completed in every nation and among every tongue, our blessed Lord and almighty King will return.   So let us labor and endure with joy "till He come."

Printed in the United States of America